100 GREAT SALES IDEAS

TITLES IN THE 100 **GREAT IDEAS** SERIES

GREAT
SALES
IDEAS

FROM LEADING COMPANIES
AROUND THE WORLD

Patrick Forsyth

CONTENTS

INTRODUCTION

God is on the side not of the heavy battalions, but of the best shots.

Voltaire

SELLING—THE PERSONAL interaction between buyer and seller—is a key part of the overall marketing process. In many businesses it is the final link. In other words whatever other marketing activity has been undertaken, from sending a brochure or mailing to running a major advertising campaign, and however much interest it has generated, selling must convert that interest—turning it into action to buy.

Sometimes the sales process consists of a single event—you talk to the customer and, all being well, they buy. On other occasions the nature of the product or service and of the customer's attitude to it means that a whole series of events must take place. These range from a simple inquiry to a series of meetings, and maybe more besides (sending a written proposal or making a presentation, for instance). Every stage is important, and whatever is done, it must be done well; the focus here is primarily on the face-to-face interaction between salespeople and customers.

The sales task is to communicate clearly and persuasively, and very often also it is to positively *differentiate* an offering from that of the competition. It is a fragile process, by which I mean that results can be changed—for good or ill—by small changes in approach. This may even go down to the use of one word rather than another, certainly to one description rather than another. Markets may be competitive, customers demanding and fickle, and selling success will not "just happen" because you have a good product or the "gift of the gab." As has been said, in today's market a key issue is to differentiate, to ensure your approach sets you apart from competition. But of one thing you can be sure:

> Selling success can be made more certain if you adopt an active approach, understand the way it works, and deploy the right techniques in the right way.

Think about any skill. Can you juggle with three flaming torches without burning holes in the carpet? Maybe not, but there are people who can. What is the difference between them and you? Perhaps only that they have thought about how to do it, understand how to go about it and have practiced doing it. Selling is no different.

The archetypal "born salesperson" is rare indeed. Good salespeople, however, are much more common. And the best of them have a secret. They understand the process of buying and selling. They adopt a conscious approach in the light of that understanding, and they deploy an approach that utilizes well-chosen techniques that are in turn well matched to each individual customer or prospect with whom they are dealing.

Sometimes what needs to be done is counterintuitive, in the way that, faced with a complaint, many people find it almost impossible to avoid making it clear that whatever happened was "not my fault" even though that is the last thing the customer wants to hear. The overall prevailing standard of salespersonship is by no means good, and there is much that is bad or at least unthinking and poorly focused on customers. Many salespeople muddle through, thinking that all that is necessary is a personable approach. If people like me they will buy from me, they say. They make sales (provided the product is good) but they will never sell as much as they could.

What does all this mean? *It means that those who tackle this area and get it right have a considerable opportunity to maximize sales results and thus positively influence the growth and profitability of the business.*

Selling is the most personal area of marketing. It is what you do that can guarantee success, what you say and how you say it. The intention of this book is to provide ideas and highlight approaches that will enable you to sharpen your sales skills and maximize the results they produce. Nothing here is dauntingly intellectually taxing. Selling—good selling—is to a large extent common sense. It is, however, a complex process. In a sales meeting that lasts even half an hour (and some last much longer), there is a great deal happening and there are many things to remember.

Furthermore, the same solution and approach is not right for every customer, much less for every occasion. Rather, you need to find appropriate ways forward literally day by day, customer by customer, and meeting by meeting. Selling is a dynamic process, and changing market situations demand a flexible approach. The best salespeople do not operate by rote, they do not "script" their presentation, and they are always conscious of the fine detail of what they do. Indeed, a specific and individual customer focus is essential to everything in the sales process, and that is a theme throughout this book. (It is inherent in the definition of selling referred to later.)

There are many individual ideas described here: things designed to make the description within your sales presentation more powerful, for instance. They range right across the sales process. They are not presented in any particular order, least of all an order of priorities, nor do they claim to include every last aspect of the sales job. Whatever they focus on, specifically there are ideas here that can be:

- Directly copied and adopted in your business.

- Adapted: fine-tuned or changed somewhat to make them fit and be useful in your business.

- Used as a catalyst, prompting a chain of thought that leads to action and a useful change of practice.

Given the dynamic nature of markets and the fickle nature of customers, selling technique must always be deployed flexibly, selecting what works where and when. Anything that creates change and prompts a development of methodology in this ongoing search for excellence can be useful. There is no single definitive "right way to sell." What matters is what works today and with a particular prospect or customer. Tomorrow or next week we may need a revised approach; next year we most certainly will.

So this book—this series—is designed to be stimulating; it is an aid to prompting ongoing review and change. It is also flexible. There is no need to read the whole book at a sitting (other than to check quickly how you might beef up your sales approaches). It can be dipped into, and as each idea is explained in a self-contained way, you can note particular ideas, think through their potential usefulness to you, and consider what action you may usefully take in light of them one by one. This keeps the process manageable, and prevents you having to try to concentrate on too much simultaneously, which would make it difficult to keep all the balls in the air at once, as it were.

Some ideas you will be able to use at once. Others may, as has been said, prompt thought that leads to action and change. Some may only be interesting, but of no immediate relevance—sometimes because you are operating that way already. No matter, the process of reading the book is likely to put you in a constructive frame of mind.

There is no magic formula to guarantee success in selling. If there is a common factor, it is that those people who are most successful at it all make a conscious effort to see it as a fluid and dynamic process: one with which they can work, adopting a style and an approach as well as deploying appropriate techniques that give them the greatest chance of success.

This book provides a resource to assist the continuous process of analysis and review that is necessary to create sales excellence.

Patrick Forsyth

THE IDEAS

THE IDEAS LED the preparation of this book. The main criteria involved in selecting them were to describe approaches that make sense—that work—and that also demonstrate a constructive and creative way of viewing the sales job. The focus is on face-to-face selling, although that might mean a member of the field sales team or a senior manager who happens to have front-line customer contact.

Many of these ideas are no doubt in use in many different organizations. With some, although they were observed in a particular organization, they may not be common, or universal, practice; it may be that what was observed represented the initiative of one creative individual. No matter, it is their usefulness that got them included.

Some ideas are in a form that links very directly to an industry or product, but that is the nature of examples. What matters is whether they can, by their nature, assist you make changes and do things differently so that sales results—whether volume or profitability—are positively affected. So do not reject an idea because it is from outside your industry, or because it is shown as being used by a large company and you represent a small one (or vice versa). Look for how the idea—or just the germ of the idea—might act to influence your business, and how precisely you might be able to draw on it to deploy an approach with your customers that they will respond to positively.

The range is intentionally eclectic. The companies specifically mentioned here include both large and small. They range from Raffles Hotel (Singapore) to Sony and Amazon. In addition, observation of other people and organizations has contributed to this review, though they are not specifically linked to one individual example. These include Cathay Pacific Airways and Waterstone's Bookshops, and others that reflect industries across a wide range of products and services. A few are from my own experience of selling, the source of others lost or protected. All can potentially teach us something.

GETTING PEOPLE TO GIVE YOU TIME

MANY SALESPEOPLE NEED to take steps to get people to give them their undivided attention, to spend sufficient time with them and to do so willingly because they believe it is useful. But . . .

People are busy, these days pressure on time seems to be greater than ever before, and anything other than a realistic attitude to this is unlikely to help you sell successfully. Clearly a more professional approachis more likely to be seen as relevant, but the more imaginative salespeople can take specific action to maximize time spent.

The idea

In a major international airline . . .

There is a particular salesperson known internally as "the donut man." Given that part of his job is to call regularly on travel agents and brief their staff on new developments (such as new routes, fares, and special offers), he has a problem. If he does this one person at a time, then even in a medium-sized city agency it could take a long time to brief everyone. The agency will not let him do it with everyone at one time—telephones must be answered and business must continue. So he has evolved a cunning plan: he arranges to see half the staff at a time, and promises to arrive "bearing gifts." At the appointed time he appears with a tray of coffees, teas, and donuts from a nearby café. Half the staff takes a break together, they gather round, and he can brief them in a convivial atmosphere. When he has finished the staff swap: the now briefed group go back on duty, and the other half take a break. They all like it. They pay attention. And they look forward to his next visit.

Most important, they are up to date, and well able to steer their customers toward this particular airline in their day-to-day work.

In practice

- Think about how your customers' businesses work and aim to fit in with their special nature.

- Sometimes something unconventional can fit this criterion and work well; stay open-minded.

2 BE AVAILABLE

It is, of course, a fact that often it is tedious dealing with customers who will not make up their mind. You want confirmation now. They want to think about it (which reminds me of the saying that when a customer says "I'll think about it and let you know"—*you know*). But what matters most is the customer's timetable, rather than the seller's. However long they mull things over for, whatever sort of gap appears between one contact and another (and there is a need here to keep in touch and take an initiative in following up), when they are ready to act, they are ready to act.

It can be galling to spend time creating interest, keeping in touch, perhaps over some time, and then finding that you lose business because you were not available when they actually wanted to say "Let's talk."

The idea

In the world-renowned Raffles Hotel in Singapore . . .

The general manager here, who certainly sees a key part of his role as selling, gives his personal cellphone number to many of his guests. Given the international nature of the business, with guests coming from time zones all over the world, this seems like a formula for a sleepless life. Not so. The number is only usually passed on personally, so the manager can judge something about the value and hazards of doing so. If it is done right, with a little description about its use, then its use is evidently not abused (well, not often!). The manager gets a few time-wasting calls at odd hours of the day, but reports that, generally speaking, it is a valuable tactic and one that "definitely produces business."

It allows contact in a way that customers see as very convenient—allowing them to make contact at the top of the hotel's organization when they want—and their being given such a number is seen as an unusual gesture, one they appreciate.

There is a direct link here for most people, one that applies to contact with an organization or an individual by phone, email and in other ways.

In practice

- Use modern technology such as the cellphone—but do not regard its use as routine, make it special.

- Be seen to "go the extra mile."

MAKE CUSTOMERS RESPECT YOU

IF A CUSTOMER sees you as professional, they will be more likely to trust you, to listen to your advice—and to buy from you.

Sometimes what can engender this respect comes through general manner and how you are with people, rather than from something that is inherently part of the sales approach. In this respect sales and service are often closely related, especially in a service business. Show signs of exemplary service and selling almost automatically becomes easier.

The idea

At a hotel in the Marriott chain . . .

During a recent stay of mine in a hotel the following occurred. Checking in, the system was that a uniformed member of staff came out from Reception, handled the paperwork quickly and efficiently as you sat in a comfortable seating area, then escorted you to your room. The women who did this for me did it efficiently and charmingly. When I was crossing Reception to check out two or three days later, the same person approached me offering help. Told I was checking out, she said, "Please let me handle this for you. It's Room 234, Mr Forsyth, isn't it?" Amazed at her memory I asked how many rooms there were in the hotel (nearly 500, she told me) and asked, "Do you remember everyone's room number?" She smiled and replied, "Yes, most of them." I believed her, and loved the fact that she so clearly enjoyed being able to say that. I immediately saw her differently.

She had the responsibility of looking after guests in a more complete manner than is usual—seeing to the whole check-in process for instance, and more no doubt besides. She is doubtless part of what persuades many guests to return, even without engaging in overt sales activity.

In practice

- Never forget how sales and service overlap, and never fail to see, and use, the service aspect as a way to provide a foundation for successful selling. That's especially true if what makes a mark can be done as delightfully as this.

A GOOD FIRST IMPRESSION

You ONLY GET one chance to make a good first impression. That statement may be a cliché, but it is true. In sales terms another maxim is almost more important: first impressions last. However you look at it, selling is easier if first impressions lead people to positive conclusions, and prompt thoughts like: that's a good start—so far so good—I like that, now what comes next?

Sometimes this can be achieved simply and it is specific to the individual; it is something they do. Sometimes, more rarely perhaps, the impression stems from the whole company, and more rarely still, it is something that achieves a real wow factor.

The idea

At international construction machinery company JCB . . .

Here is a company that certainly wows first-time visitors to its factory in the English Midlands, especially those who come from overseas. Its product needs demonstrating so it no doubt has visitors aplenty. Imagine: you fly from wherever—Peru or Paris—and even if you are not familiar with the country, you know that the place you will visit is a significant journey from London. (You imagine the usual hazards of any journey—traffic, hold-ups and so on.) But your hosts say they will meet you at Heathrow Airport, London, so that sounds a little easier.

Then the meeting turns out to be a brief connection to the company helicopter and a very straightforward direct flight, of only an hour or so, which lands you in the landscaped grounds surrounding the factory.

Not everyone can run to a company helicopter, but attention to any detail at first contact that will give the right impression is worthwhile and helps set the scene for the subsequent meeting. The helicopter may be a dramatic way of doing things, but it is really only one way of providing extra service and convenience to customers. This is true of the individual, several individuals, or the organization itself.

In practice

- Seek to make genuine service, rather than gimmicks, enhance customer acceptance.

- Ensure that there are management processes to consider/ approve expenditure on such things (though not necessarily of this magnitude!).

ENHANCING CUSTOMERS' RECALL OF YOU

HERE IS A card trick that creates a positive, and lasting, impression. A smart business card is part of the basic kit of anyone selling. In some markets (in the East for instance, where the Japanese even have plastic waterproof cards to exchange by the pool), their existence and use is especially important, and they may have a translation of the information on the back.

But cards can all look much the same. Just glance at your store of those from other people—better still, put yours among them and see if it stands out. So something that is truly distinctive may be worthwhile. One tactic used by some organizations is for people to have their photograph on their card. (It can be color or black and white, and is in some cases a line drawing—I have seen cartoons and caricatures too.) Here is a different idea.

The idea

From FMC Southeast Asia Pte Ltd (a firm in the undersea technologies sector) . . .

One manager with this company always gives people two cards. They are printed on a card of a shape you may be familiar with as an example of an optical illusion (see opposite). When two cards are put down one above the other, one seems clearly to be the larger. Put them one on top of another and it is clear they are identical in size. It is of no significance other than as a bit of fun; but it is memorable.

I have another card, a tiny 6 × 4 cm, which has only a picture of someone on the front, the words CALL ME, and a telephone number. On the reverse side it says, "The lack of business from you has made this economy-sized card necessary." That idea is maybe not for everyone, but why not have several different cards if they are useful?

In practice

- Review any sort of standard printed material regularly. Do not think of it as fixed and unalterable.

- Then find formats that work for you and your customers.

ENHANCING CUSTOMERS' RECALL OF YOU (CONTINUED)

A BUSINESS CARD certainly acts as a reminder of you, especially early on in a relationship with a customer. It is something that is likely to be kept, and it demands an active step to get rid of it, when the customer thinks, I shan't want to contact them. But how do you boost such a positive effect when time passes and memory dims?

The idea

A host of organizations do this badly . . .

A momentary boost to the memory, your profile, and the relationship can be created by giving a gift. First, beware of being seen to offer a bribe. It is one thing to give something as a thank you to someone who buys regularly from you, but some people might think too much too soon sends the wrong messages, so some care is necessary.

Some care is needed too in selecting something appropriate. Beware, some things fall flat for reasons like these:

- It's too late. The traditional diary given just before Christmas is a case in point. I have lost count of the ones I have received over the years, and I have never used them. I always have a diary on the go by the time the gift arrives.

- It's gone in a flash. A bottle of scotch or some wine may be appreciated, but it doesn't last. It'll be gone by Boxing Day, and it doesn't surprise anyone.

- It's tacky. No more splodgy ballpoint pens please.

What is needed is something that is distinctive, useful, and perhaps unusual. For instance, I carry my business cards in a leather case that was this kind of gift (thank you, Marriott Hotels). It is a good example of an item that is likely to be kept even if someone has something similar already. As an example of something useful and more unusual, my book *Successful Time Management* (Kogan Page) has several times been purchased by companies and used in this way. Showing you are aware the buyer is busy may be just what you need. (How many copies would you like? Sorry, but if a book on selling can't contain a few plugs, what can?)

In practice

- Think about appropriate small gifts, and plan sufficiently far ahead to take creative action.

- Ring the changes: use something different every year.

FIND THE DECISION MAKER

ANY SELLING TECHNIQUE must be directed to the decision maker, whoever that is (it may be more than one person). Identifying who you are talking to and what role they play is vital. Sometimes your contact will have a specific brief: perhaps they are a "recommender," asked by a decision maker to check things out. If you feel other people are involved in the buying decision, you need to engineer a link to them, or better still a meeting with them.

The idea

From a major Volvo car dealer . . .

It is said that the most important thing in selling a car is to get the prospect to sit in the driver's seat, with taking a test drive coming a close and linked second. So far so good, but what happens when you have identified that a family is involved and yet only one of the key players comes to the dealership? This might be either a male or female partner, and who is to say which of the pair is the more important? Once you have persuaded this person to take a test drive, one ploy that can be used here is to organize the route so that in its latter stages it goes close to the prospect's home. (This assumes they live within reach, but most likely they do, or why would they go into that dealership?) Then as the drive is nearing completion the salesperson suggests a stop at the house, using an appropriate phrase such as "Let your wife have a look."

This creates a meeting within a meeting. Suddenly the salesperson has both halves of the decision-making duo together, and can tackle the remaining stage of the sale with both of them. All being well, the drive will already have made a good impression, and seeing the car parked on their own driveway helps stimulate the prospects' imagination.

This is a novel response to the problem of involving all decision makers. It is well tailored to the way such sales work, and uses a suggestion that is likely to be seen only as a helpful addition to what is being done.

In practice

- Always explore and identify who the true decision maker is for your prospect, and remember the decision may involve several people.

- Make your sales approach suit, and if possible be special to, all the people involved.

CLOSE CONTACT

MANY CUSTOMERS CHECK out potential purchases on the internet these days. This means that by the time someone makes contact with an individual business they have done their research and may see the process of selection and buying as well on the way. But this can create long-distance contacts from customers who are not physically near the salesperson. There's a good side to this: it exposes salespeople to prospects with whom they would never otherwise have had any contact. But how do you get closer?

The idea

From a Volvo dealership . . .

One industry in which this internet checking now goes on is car sales, including secondhand ones. People can check out possibilities and prices, and when they have an idea of the kind of car they want, they can see a list of every car for sale in the country that meets their exact criteria and where it is to be found. Then they can contact the appropriate dealer, who may be on the other side of the country. At that point they want to hear about the car, gleaning details beyond the basic description of year, color, and so on. If they are still interested, they will doubtless resolve to go and have a look at it.

One salesperson I spoke to in my local Volvo dealership has cracked this one. He offers to drive the car to the prospect (or maybe to meet them halfway). This surprises people, and that surprise helps him gauge the seriousness of their intent. This is important because a journey costs time and money, but if he is confident he's found a good prospect, then it can pay dividends. Indeed my informant claims a good strike rate. After all, he does not suggest this to anyone he suspects of time wasting.

In practice

- Review how e-marketing is affecting the way your customers behave. (It will likely be changing and need regular review.)

- Adapt your approach to fit with their new practice.

THE RIGHT WEIGHT OF CASE

A DIFFICULTY SOME salespeople have is in deciding how much to say about their product or service. Realistically comprehensiveness is often not one of the options: more and more buyers lay down time restraints in one way or another. You might sensibly regard such a time limit as negotiable, but once you have agreed it there is merit in sticking to it, unless the prospect is so interested that they extend it, either formally or informally. Beyond that pragmatic view, however, how do you judge how much to say?

The idea

From research done by m62 visualcommunications ltd . . .

Most of the ideas suggested here are based as much as anything on observation, but this one is based on research. This company specializes in helping create business-winning presentations (deciding on the message and creating the visual aids to convey it). In this capacity its staff must judge carefully how much to suggest is said, not least because they can be paid in part on results. So they did some research into the "weight of a case."

The answer was clear. The greatest chance of a positive reaction is given by five key points stated in benefit form. Do not take that too literally: you may do well by using four or six, or even seven points. But outside these parameters you risk a negative reaction. Too few points, and the case will sound insubstantial; too many, and it will become tedious and people will lose interest. Of course, quantity is not everything. Naturally it matters what you say and how you say it, and what priority you give to different points. But there is guidance here, and it is worth thinking in this way about the core of your message—the case you want to present. Although the research was directed primarily at "big-ticket" selling, and situations where a formal pitch and presentation is necessary, common sense suggests that it is a good general point to bear in mind.

Note: the research is described in Nick Oulton's *Killer Presentations* (How To Books), which also outlines the best methodology you could wish for in creating persuasive PowerPoint presentations.

In practice

- The case you make easily becomes repetitive if you don't give it thought. So analyze what you say, and make sure it has sufficient "weight" in the kind of way described above.

10. DON'T WASTE CUSTOMERS' TIME

We all know people are busy these days. Customers normally take what they consider an appropriate amount of time to make a decision. So it makes sense not to try to sidestep that, by either rushing them or spinning out the sale. That's especially true if they don't see the extra time taken as useful, and it's worse if they see the process as unnecessarily and uncaringly lengthy.

The idea

From book publishers Bantam Press . . .

Sometimes the time a salesperson is allowed must be agreed upfront, and sometimes too it needs to be negotiated. A salesperson must try to get time to make the planned pitch, and a customer must accept that if they want to make an informed decision, they must listen to key information about the product or service. The key point here is to respect the time customers have available, then actively work on descriptions, indeed your whole pitch, to ensure that you can make a powerful case in the time available.

In some industries people are under more time pressure than in others, and the unremitting nature of that pressure means that salespeople have to consider this or they simply cannot do the job. One example is publishing. Large publishers not only have hundreds or thousands of titles in print, they add dozens of new ones every month. A salesperson selling to retail bookshops has to find a way of being strikingly succinct. Some titles may be dealt with in a minute or less. Some years ago when Stephen Hawking's surprise bestseller *A Brief History of Time* was selling in its millions, I asked salespeople on a publishing industry sales training course to pick a title to describe, first without time pressure, then with a tight cut-off time. When we came to the succinct version, a representative from Bantam Press simply held up Hawking's book and gave a four-word sales pitch: "It's now in paperback."

Sometimes circumstances make this easy, but even when they don't, the principle stands. You must not risk wasting customers' time. Working out truly succinct, yet powerful, descriptions is a certain aid to sales success.

In practice

- It can be easy to spend longer with customers than they find ideal, because they might not tell you so.

- So ask about timing. It will be regarded as a courtesy. Then you can fit your pitch to their timescale and get their full attention throughout.

BE ON TIME

PUNCTUALITY IS ONE of the old-fashioned virtues. It is in the same mold as courtesy, of which we are told that it "costs nothing." Both matter, and punctuality links to a thought already expressed here, that you should not waste a customer's time. If you are asked to turn up at 10am or whatever, do so. Organize yourself so that you can. This means everything from leaving sufficient time for a journey, to finding out in advance where you will be able to park. Don't waste 10 minutes driving around in circles, then arrive late, mouthing the old cliché about awful traffic. You may get away with it, but it makes a difference. If things are finely balanced, it's something to put on the negative side when your offering is weighed up.

The idea

From a small replacement tire specialist . . .

A salesperson selling tires to construction companies with fleets of huge trucks and road-building equipment had been after one particular prospect for a while. He was put off many times, then the prospect finally agreed to a meeting. They specified 8am, and phrased it as, "Be there on time. It's the only chance you'll get." Their location meant he had a three-hour drive, so this meant a very early start. It would have been very easy to beg for a later meeting, or turn up late regardless.

He did not do that. He agreed with gratitude, rose at the crack of dawn and drove the distance, breakfasting on the way. He sat down in the prospect's reception area with about 10 minutes in hand. The meeting went well, the firm placed an initial order, and at the end of the meeting (the reason I was told about this, and remember it) the customer said something like this. "I must apologize for getting you here so early. I know you must have had a very early start, but if we're going to deal with you I have to be sure of your commitment to service. Next time let's have lunch."

It was, unashamedly, a test. If he had complained about the timing or been late, he might never have received an order from what became a regular and significant customer.

In practice

- Be punctual. It could be worth more than you think.

- Recognize tests for what they are, and maybe set some too. They relate to a basic customer need for reassurance.

INSISTING ON RESPECT

THE RELATIONSHIP BETWEEN a customer and a supplier is worth some thought. The people involved do not have to like each other, at least not in the "Do come to dinner" sense, but they must have a good working relationship. There must be trust that the supplier will do as they say—or promise—and there must to a degree be mutual respect. The latter can be achieved in a number of ways, many of them linked to service and what is done.

The idea

This one is from my own experience . . .

I was in discussion with a potential client that was considering commissioning some training work. A meeting went well, and was followed by my submitting a written proposal. Another meeting was scheduled. I arrived, as I try to do, a few minutes early and announced myself at the reception. The appointed time—10am— came and went. At 10:20 I spoke to the receptionist, to make sure my arrival had been announced. I was assured it had.

At 10:30am, with no word from my prospect (not even the offer of a cup of tea!), I wrote a short note that I left with the receptionist. It explained that I had other appointments and could wait no more, but I hoped we would be able to reschedule the meeting. I told the receptionist what it said, and asked her to pass it on. It was some 40 minutes after the appointment time when I left. It only took me half an hour to be back at my desk. I was met by both an email and a voicemail message apologizing, and asking for the meeting to be rescheduled soon.

The point here is that I told a white lie. In fact I could have waited longer, but I chose not to. I had met the people concerned, and was able to judge their level of interest. I knew, or thought I did, the sort of relationship that was developing. I certainly knew how I wanted to be perceived. I felt I had more to gain by leaving than by waiting meekly until they saw fit to see me.

Certainly a judgment and an element of risk are involved here, but in this case it worked. Another meeting was swiftly arranged. It started with more apologies—from both sides. I said I was sorry to have left, but had not wanted to let someone else down. It ended with a firm date set for the course in question.

In practice

- Customer focus does not imply subservience, so actively position yourself as someone with professional clout.

- Fit such action carefully to individual customers.

BE WILLING TO GET YOUR HANDS DIRTY

Not all sales meetings take place in a cozy office, or indeed in any sort of comfortable environment. Some take place on the move, some are conducted outdoors, I've known them to happen at the bottom of a mineshaft. The environment and the circumstances provide opportunities for salespeople, but sometimes it takes a moment to organize yourself to fit them.

When I started out in consultancy and training, the company I worked with did a great deal of work for agricultural machinery producers Massey Ferguson. It became a regular trick that when a new consultant started work on the account, no one told them to put a pair of Wellington boots in their car. More than one person found themselves out and about on various farms floundering in inches of mud (or worse) in their best shoes as a result. Of course, salespeople with experience of that industry knew a pair of boots was a standard part of the kit.

The idea

From a company manufacturing road sweepers . . .

The reason for putting boots in the car was not just to keep clean, but also to be able to suggest and respond to opportunities to see things at first hand. I once watched a salesperson supervising the demonstration of a motorized street cleaner, a little vehicle with twin brushes at the front, to a town council committee. A driver was operating the machine, and the salesperson was giving the assembled group a running commentary about what was happening.

At one point the machine hit some stubborn weeds growing in the crack between the sidewalk and a building. The salesperson pulled an overall out of his briefcase, donned it over his business suit, and walked over to the machine. He took a spade off a rack at the back of the vehicle and loosened the weeds, which the brushes then picked up with no problem. He returned to the group and seamlessly linked what he had done to the operation of the machine with a two-man team in certain areas.

I remember this because after this demonstration, and a demonstration of another competing machine, the chair of the committee asked its members which they favored. No one spoke, so he gave us his own opinion. "I'll tell you what I think, I bet the service from X is best. I like a man who's prepared to get his hands dirty."

The principle here is certainly an idea that can impress and enhance the strength of a sales pitch.

In practice

- Analyze your typical sales encounter to see how you can include an element of "getting your hands dirty" within it, either physically or metaphorically.

LOSE YOUR EGO

IN MANY FIELDS of selling it is more important to get the order than to get the credit or some kind of personal involvement.

The idea

A consulting firm (which must remain nameless) . . .

Without a doubt the best example I have ever come across of this occurred in a training consultancy. A potential project had reached a crucial stage. An inquiry had been received, meetings held, and a written proposal submitted. Everything seemed to be going well, and at his most confident, the consultant who had achieved this much believed that confirmation was imminent. Indeed he soon got a response, but it was negative.

In many bespoke businesses the next step is to try to find out why the company hasn't won the contract. If you can do so—in this case it might have involved price, method, timing, a less than favorable comparison with an alternative supplier, or many more reasons— this can be useful information for the future.

Sometimes such a discovery call can actually change things and turn a no into a yes, as happened this time. The consultant telephoned the decision maker and persuaded him to discuss why the company had said no. However he was not very forthcoming. Various reasons were floated but there was nothing substantial, nothing that seemed to be the key factor. Reading between the lines, the consultant opted for bluntness. "I think I know what the problem is," he said. "You don't like me." There was a long silence and then the prospect agreed!

This is not something most clients would want to say unprompted. But not only did the consultant find out the reason, he turned the situation around. He persuaded the client to meet a younger colleague and consider giving her the job. She got it.

In practice

- We cannot all get on with everyone to the same extent. Beyond that, the principle of checking on the reasons for a refusal is eminently worthwhile.

- So too is an approach that does not take too egocentric an approach to things.

15 | CLIMB THE STAIRS

MANY BUSINESSES NEED a constant supply of new prospects. Prospecting—and cold calling—is not most salespeople's favorite activity. The trick to ensuring that you have a constant supply of new people to talk to is to have a number of methods, where each lends itself to regularly producing some new names. These might include everything from combing directories or association membership lists to simple observation—who's moving into that new building under construction.

The idea

I first observed this being done by the representative of a printing firm . . .

Any salesperson has to create personal effectiveness in terms of time. Prospecting must not take too long, and you do not want to undertake labyrinthine research when something simpler will do the job. The salesperson I am thinking of here worked in central London. He wanted to find customers within a tight radius of the printing works to minimize travel time, and had hit on what he called the climbing stairs method of prospecting. This he did specifically to try to find new customers close to existing ones.

Every time he visited a customer in an office block, he took the stairs (on the way down is easiest!) and checked out what other organizations were operating in the building. If he found a likely prospect, it only took a moment to nip in and ask a few questions at reception. Occasionally he met a decision maker as a result. More often he got information and names, and could make a more considered approach later. It was a very time-effective method. The same sort of thing can be made to work in a variety of different circumstances, for example on an industrial estate. Sometimes the notice listing occupants in the lobby is helpful, but actually seeing the front door or going in allows a better judgment to be made about potential.

In practice

- Anything like this can be made a habit. Something that takes little time but can be done regularly day after day is especially useful.

- Prospecting is as much a question of attitude as of technique. Those who think about it positively are rarely short of someone new to talk to.

16 STRAWBERRIES AND CREAM

One sure way to sell more is to link selling one thing to selling another. This is true from a marketing perspective—for example cellphones and call revenue, or computer printers and toner cartridges—but it is also true of selling. Historically, for obvious reasons, it has been known as the strawberries and cream technique.

The idea

Check out the Amazon website . . .

The way to make this idea work is to envisage links between one thing and another, or better still one thing and a whole raft of others. The past masters of this are Amazon. Visit the Amazon website and notice how it is set up. Whatever you do on it—just view something, add it to a wish list, or buy it—the system makes use of what you appear interested in to make other suggestions to you.

For example, if you're looking at books, it will provide links based on the author, the kind of book, the subject of non-fiction titles, and more. That the system works well in terms of human psychology is demonstrated by how addictive it is. As a habitual book buyer I can spend a long time following a track through the system to see if it puts something interesting, unknown, and perhaps surprising in front of me.

It is worth examining your own product range to see how different things can be made to link together. Bear in mind that some links will be obvious, but others will not. All that matters is that there is a logic that is recognized by the customer. Linking purchases can save time and hassle: so someone selling paper to an office might also offer spare cartridges for the printer (among other things). Paper is, after all, not much use without ink.

This technique can link effectively to others. For example, some companies vary prices on the basis of combinations of product, so paper might be offered at a lower price to those customers buying a toner cartridge, or depending on the quantity ordered. Now just to practice what I preach, let me suggest that if you bought this book, maybe you would also find another one helpful. If you want something on how to excel in your career, look no further: *Detox Your Career* by Patrick Forsyth (Cyan/Marshall Cavendish Books) is readily available.

In practice

- Again regular analysis is necessary here.

- This makes a useful topic for sales meetings, when different combinations can be explored or exchanged.

USE VISUAL AIDS EVEN WHEN YOU CANNOT

EVERY SALESPERSON KNOWS the truth of the old saying that a picture is worth a thousand words. Visual aids (everything from a graph to the product itself) have to be used in the right way. You must let them speak for themselves, and that means keeping quiet once they have been introduced and shown. (This is typically not something that salespeople find easy to do, but people cannot concentrate on taking in what they see and listening at the same time, so if you talk, they might miss a point and your case will be diluted.)

The idea

This comes from the world of mining . . .

The way to make the best of visual aids is not simply to see what is available and use it, whether it's appropriate or not. It is to see what *could* be useful and organize whatever is necessary to make it available. A salesperson selling mining equipment made this point strongly to me. He sold machines like a Black & Decker drill but the size of a small car. It was not practical to bring a machine along to someone's office, and it was difficult to get potential buyers to go and look at machines until he had generated some interest.

This salesperson carried a large and very heavy pilot's case to his first meetings with prospects. Inside was a piece of granite. (He had a nice story about how it was formed millions of years ago and came from the Grampian Mountains in Scotland.) One side of it had been cut by the machine, as easily as a knife would go through butter, judging by how flat and shiny it was. It provided dramatic evidence of the power and precision of the equipment, and was doubly effective in making its point because, given the nature of the machinery, prospects were not expecting to see anything.

In practice

- If necessary you must contrive or invent something that will do the visual job you want, that will stimulate a prospect's imagination. Of course, the first task is to decide what role the visual can usefully play.

- Even when what is sold is not very visual, the same principle applies. For example, I saw an accountancy firm increase the sales of audits to small/medium-sized businesses by producing a double-sized set of accounts. This could then be shown to prospects with a commentary about what they could do with the information they contained (for example, better manage their cash flow).

MAKE PAYMENT DEPENDENT ON RESULTS

Buying anything entails some risk. Customers wonder, will it be good, will it work, and will it last? And will I regret buying it? Understandably, if something is seen as expensive, these sorts of feeling are intensified. People tend to worry less if they see something as good value, or are offered a special deal. But there is another way to reduce their perception of risk.

The idea

This idea comes from m62 visualcommunications (and others) . . .

One sure way to change the perception of both risk and price is to offer a price linked to results or satisfaction. I mentioned this company on page 24: it specializes in creating high-powered persuasive presentations for organizations involved in big-ticket selling. Some would say its services are expensive, although its results are impressive. With certain kinds of client situation it offers a results-based price: if the presentation it creates is designed to win a specific piece of business or contract, there is a reduction in price if the bid is unsuccessful. So in a sense, it asks for a higher price if all goes well or a lower one if it does not.

Clearly a supplier doing this has to be confident in the satisfaction it delivers, and there is often an element of risk too. In this example m62 cannot control the circumstances in which its clients make their pitch, or exactly how they do it. But the salesperson able to offer this certainly creates both novelty and differentiation.

This technique is used by many businesses. I have seen it in circumstances as different as a restaurant (you pay what you think the meal was worth, which is actually what most customers do with regard to a tip), consultative services, and a motivational speaker.

In practice

- One caveat: there needs to be a considered and organized policy here. Precedents can be set. The deal for one customer may upset another (and yes, others will get to know), so an individual salesperson should check before initiating such an offer in isolation.

19 SUPPORT THEIR CHARITY

THERE ARE PARTS of the world where bribes are the norm, but for the most part it is not a good idea to bribe your prospect, and certainly that is not one of the ideas listed here. However, there are ways to please people that cannot be categorized as bribes. One is to support a charity favored by a prospect or customer.

The idea

From an Australian professional body . . .

I came across this at the time of the Boxing Day tsunami in Southeast Asia. On a visit to Australia I was keen to put my time to profitable use, and suggested to a number of local bodies that I gave a talk or seminar during my visit. One organization that took up the offer was involved in raising money for tsunami victims, and it was agreed that some of the money from the event would go to that cause. I supported this charity particularly because I had been on holiday in Thailand in the aftermath of the event, so I was happy to do this. It made a favorable impression even before I had met anyone from the association.

Other possibilities can utilize the same principle. For example a financial adviser might invite people to a day's golf (yes, some business really is done on the golf course), but to play in a competition that is designed to raise money for a good cause. This gives people an additional reason to agree, and gives the adviser the chance for a leisurely chat with them.

Such activity has little to do with selling the product, and it is certainly not the solution to every sales problem (or charity fundraising problem). But there are circumstances where it is an excellent way of establishing or building relationships. Increasing the opportunity to talk to people in this way could lead to something more tangible. It might be used on a one-off or an ongoing basis.

In practice

- If you pursue this idea, remember that the cause or charity should appeal to the customer (and not be your pet area).

- Do not overuse this technique, or it might quickly be resented.

20 USE A SPOKEN LOGO

THERE ARE MANY circumstances when it is advantageous to be able to describe to people what you do and what you sell briefly in a sentence. One common occasion is when you meet someone at a conference and they ask, "What do you do?" If you waffle at such a moment you lose any chance of creating interest, and maybe a specific opportunity to do business.

The idea

This idea comes from the book *Why Entrepreneurs Should Eat Bananas* by Simon Tupman (Cyan/Marshall Cavendish Books), a valuable selection of ideas for "growing your business and yourself." Simon Tupman, who runs Simon Tupman Presentations, is a motivational speaker and author.

He coined the phrase "spoken logo" as an antidote to perhaps unwittingly bland and bald descriptions such as "I am a lawyer," "We make electronic equipment," and "We conduct market research." Simon quotes one of his customers, an accountant, who replies to this question with, "I take the hassle out of keeping books and records up to date for busy people who have better things to do." This is a good example because it gets straight to the point, focuses on the benefit for clients rather than the service provided, and encapsulates a good deal very succinctly.

Along the same lines, that lawyer (if he or she works in conveyancing) might say, "I take the hassle out of buying and selling a house, and make sure there are no hidden surprises." The market researcher might say, "I reduce the risk in people's businesses, and help identify market opportunities that can boost profit." Such statements are designed to prompt a useful exchange rather than a simple conversation-stopping remark like "Oh really." They also convey sufficient information that if there is any common ground that could lead to a business opportunity, they'll help to identify it.

In practice

- Finding a phrase like this off the top of your head is difficult, so give it some prior thought. Think about your business, and develop (and keep updated) a clear spoken logo. It will stand you in good stead in a variety of networking and other situations. It can be a route into a more detailed conversation that allows some real selling.

SEND A CARD

THERE IS ALWAYS a need to keep in touch, to remind customers and prospects of your continued existence, either because there is time ahead of an order or because you need to maintain contact between orders. In this electronic age the written message is going out of style, but for many people a written message still has something special about it. Indeed maybe that is precisely because it has become rarer these days.

The idea

From Highgate House Conference Centre . . .

The traditional time to send cards is at Christmas, or, in parts of Asia, at New Year. This may be something you do almost as a reflex, but have you ever stopped to think about what benefit you get from it? A typical customer may get 20, 30, even 100 cards from suppliers and business contacts ahead of Christmas. They appear in the last hectic fortnight before the holiday, and are cleared away by the office cleaner before people return to work in the New Year. Can you remember even by mid-January who sent you a card and who did not? Most likely not.

So one school of thought suggests that you should forget Christmas cards, or send something quickly and easily in email form, recognizing that it will not have any real lasting effect. On the other hand other sorts of cards are noticed much more, and may be worth sending. These include cards for someone's birthday, for anniversaries (national, personal or corporate), from your holiday, or as a taster of some news. By acting in an unusual way and sending something unexpected, but likely to be appreciated, you will make more of a mark. If the card contains a specific reminder, people are then more likely to ensure the information is noted.

One card that led to this thought was a holiday postcard from a consultant with whom I have collaborated in the past. It reminded me about a conversation I want to have with them when they return, and is stuck up beside my desk to prompt me to do just that.

In practice

- Check the diary and plan ahead.

- If you have special cards printed, make them suitable and memorable (standard material may dilute the impact).

22 DIRECT THE MEETING

It is without a doubt easiest to sell successfully if you are in the driving seat. Being too circumspect at the start can seem like a soft, comfortable approach, but it may only succeed in putting the customer in the driving seat. From there they sometimes dictate what happens, at worst with pointed questions such as "Before we do anything else, tell me what this is going to cost." You need a way to take control.

The idea

From a financial adviser . . .

Quite simply, set an agenda. Let me be more specific: suggest the agenda that you want and that you feel will make being persuasive easiest, while still making the other person feel the meeting is useful to them. First think through how you feel something is best dealt with. Have it clear in your mind (and put it in writing for more formal meetings). Then table it in a way that presumes it will be accepted. "It may well be helpful to have an agenda in mind, not least so we can do this in a reasonable time. Perhaps I could suggest . . ." In other words put it over as something that both of you will find useful. Even if it is only three items—"Let's take X first and then talk about Y and Z"—this is a powerful technique. Especially if you put forward a longer list, this might prompt counter-suggestions that mean you have to compromise a little. But simply taking the initiative means that your suggestions will often be agreed wholesale.

The result is that you can then take things in the order you want. Furthermore, once the agenda is agreed, you can introduce things progressively, presenting them not as what you want, but rather as what the prospect wants (or at least has agreed to). So you should say, "What we agreed to take next was . . ." rather than something that starts with the word "I."

In practice

- In this way you can ensure that you run the kind of meeting you want, because it is the best route to a sale, and yet one that the prospect finds they like, because it is efficient.

- If you do it well, the sales technique involved here seems like nothing more than efficiency designed to help the customer. Perfect.

REMEMBER THAT IT IS A COMMERICIAL TRANSACTION

ANY SALESPERSON HAS a complex job to do. It may run from finding prospects to conversations, meetings, written proposals, and more, but the final stage is always the same—closing on a profitable deal. But is there more to be done?

The idea

A long time ago in what is now HarperCollins, the publishing company . . .

No apologies for including this idea, even though it goes back to an early part of my career when I worked in publishing. It was there that I got into sales and marketing for the first time, although I started out wearing an editorial hat. I received a timeless piece of advice from my sales manager, which has stood me in good stead ever since. I found it especially useful when, years later, I started my own business.

I went into his office one day swelling with pride at having obtained my largest order yet. I did receive some praise, I think, but what I really remember is that he stopped me as I was halfway out of his office. "Hang on," he said. "There's something else." Then he said something that has stuck in my mind ever since. "Do remember that it's not an order until the money is in the bank."

That was wise advice, because an order for which payment is never received is worse than useless. And one where it costs a fortune to collect the payment long after delivery is made, tying up time and preventing other matters from being attended to, is not much better. As the sales process proceeds, all the things that make for prompt payment are crucial.

In practice

- Any checks (especially financial ones) must be completed thoroughly.

- A clear explanation of terms and conditions is always necessary.

- Prompt, accurate, and efficient documentation completes matters neatly.

- Meaningful, and if necessary persistent, chasing must be done if there is any delay.

- If the right attitude to payment is taken throughout the process and this truism is borne in mind, then the business will likely be more profitable in the long term.

MAKE YOUR CUSTOMER IMPROVE YOUR PRODUCTIVITY

For ANYONE SELLING, and certainly for a full-time salesperson, sales productivity is vital. Only when you are face to face with a customer or prospect will you produce business, yet there is so much more to be done. Tasks ranging from administration to traveling (and details like finding somewhere to park) take up time and, if unchecked, reduce your productivity.

The idea

From a financial adviser based in the City of London . . .

I regularly receive telephone calls from financial advisers (don't we all?), and one sticks very much in my mind. He was interesting and personable, and I listened for longer than I might have done with someone less good. I already had an adviser I was happy with, however, and did not want to pursue matters with him. But I did ask him what would happen next should I be interested. "You come and see me," he said. This surprised me. Most such people cannot wait to come to my home or office, so I queried it. "Don't you mean *you* come and see *me*?" When he confirmed that I must visit him, I explained my interest, and asked him why he used this tactic.

He explained that, first, he was concerned to maximize his productivity. "I spend time on the telephone and I spend time with prospects and clients," he said, "but I spend no time traveling, parking or sitting in other people's reception areas." Second, he was concerned to identify the best prospects. "Only those with real interest will take the time and trouble to visit me." In addition, he found that the tactic differentiated him from other advisers. "Even before I meet people they have an impression of me that helps me. They are intrigued and interested, and arrive prepared to listen," he commented.

He added that it was partly because he was based in central London and dealing with clients within easy reach of his office that this system worked well for him. He had been top salesperson in the company three years running. Of course, some prospects will have no truck with this, but enough liked it to make his approach effective—and his productivity, and thus his sales results, high.

In practice

- Never fear trying radically different ideas (although you may sensibly test them first).

- Assisting customers' productivity always goes down well, but keep tight control of your own productivity too.

25 ADOPT THE RIGHT ATTITUDE

SALESPEOPLE OFTEN ASK me what the key to sales success is. Would that it was so simple! Success comes not from one thing, but is largely in the details: the approach, the techniques used—and the attitude that people take to it. This is more than just the ubiquitous "positive mental attitude" beloved of many a book on how to be successful (in selling or anything else). It comprises a number of attitudes, including:

- A conscious and considered awareness of the psychology of selling and how it works. The best salespeople always seem to have a clear understanding of what they are doing and of deploying the right approaches at the right moment.

- A customer focus: because the psychology of decision making and buying demands this and it is a foundation for success.

- A will to win and an ability to not allow any rejection along the way to cramp their style. As few (if any) salespeople have a 100 percent strike rate this is simply necessary.

- Persistence: because not every order comes easily or instantly.

- Creativity: even a superficial reading of this book shows the need for that.

- An awareness that selling is a dynamic process. It cannot be done by rote in the same way forever. What works for one person today may need to be done differently for someone else next week, certainly next year. Good salespeople keep their approaches updated.

There are no doubt more, though some will stem from those listed. Attitudes underpin action, so how we think about things is as important as what is done. Thus it is helpful if you have habits that act to remind you of the attitudes you should adopt and maintain.

The idea

In computer giant IBM . . .

All I want to stress here is one aspect of the power of attitude, which is given weight by being favored by such a large, well-known organization. According to marketing guru Philip Kotler, a maxim used in every IBM internal training course is that whoever a salesperson is talking to, they should conduct the meeting as if they are about to lose the order. Holding such a thought will help strengthen everything that is done, making it thorough and maximizing persuasiveness.

In practice

- Identify those attitudes you can usefully display.

- Work at displaying them (this may go beyond your natural persona).

STAND UP TO CUSTOMERS

THERE IS AN old saying that if you appear to be like a doormat, you should expect people to walk all over you. Sometimes a customer relationship can feel like this. Some customers are not just demanding (aren't they all?) but take extreme liberties that demand something that goes beyond any definition of even excellent service. Such a relationship is costly, at worst reducing or removing the profitability of the business.

The idea

Seen in a market research company in Hong Kong . . .

Situated in Hong Kong, this company has offices and clients around the Asian region. At one time the staff of one of its largest clients were causing the manager they dealt with considerable problems. The clients' disorganization was at the root of the problem. They were forever canceling or changing meetings and demanding attendance at others at short notice. They commonly telephoned demanding that the manager rush to one of their many regional offices at a moment's notice, with the need to travel from, say, Hong Kong to Singapore compounding the problem. This sort of situation costs time and money, and ultimately threatened the viability of a carefully costed project. Being sales and service oriented, the manager's instinct was to respond helpfully, to manage somehow to accommodate them. In this case this just compounded the problem.

The client was of the "give us an inch and we'll take a mile and a half" school (aren't they all? you may say again). Every helpful act simply made them feel that anything demanded would be responded to positively. Ultimately, if demands go up and up, something must be done. But it is a question of degree. Where do you draw the line? Perhaps the best answer is sooner rather than later, despite the instinct to help on each individual occasion, and the real fear that saying "No" will jeopardize the client relationship.

In this case a line was drawn. The manager said "No" to a particularly inconvenient request, and reminded the clients of the terms of the assignment. Surprise, surprise—the clients, who clearly understood what they had been doing, respected his refusal and began to act differently. Profitability returned. The client relationship was improved. More assignments were booked.

In practice

- Sometimes the right thing to do is to stand up to customers.

- The trick is to decide when and how powerfully you need to react.

TACKLE A NEW CATEGORY OF CUSTOMER

However experienced you are, you may find yourself faced with selling in circumstances where you have no experience, indeed no frame of reference, and where the nature of a business area and those in it are to a degree alien. It is a mistake to think that if you can sell one thing successfully, you can sell everything and anything. Your lack of experience may show and blight the results you want.

The idea

From consultant and author Frances Kay . . .

This is another example from my personal experience. First, let me say that most people who write books—business books, at any rate—do so at least in part because it is visible and helps build a positive profile. Frances Kay agreed with this. She wanted to add a book to her credentials, but was unsure how to go about selling the idea to a suitable publisher. This is a specialist area, and probably hundreds of proposals are received for every single book that is published, so the strike rate can be low. So she looked around for someone who had been published and presumably gone through the necessary learning curve.

She settled on me (I have written more than 50 books), and made contact to set up a meeting. I was able to give her a crash course in how to approach, pitch an idea, and deal with a publisher. This certainly saved her significant time, and allowed her to make a much more precise and suitable approach than she might otherwise have done. (She says this, I am trying not to blow my own trumpet here.) She subsequently had her book on networking, *Brilliant Business Connections*, published (by How To Books), and an excellent book it is too. She has gone on to write a number of other titles, including *New Kid on the Block* (published by Cyan/Marshall Cavendish Books), about how to deal with the first moments on taking up a new job.

In practice

- The principle here is clear: there is no point in trying to reinvent the wheel if you can liaise with someone who has done so already, and extend your sales approach through acquiring something of their experience.

CHALLENGE THE CUSTOMER'S CULTURE

A NUMBER OF the ideas described here are effective not only because they are practical in one way or another, but also because they do something that customers find unexpected. This element alone is worth considering: it's useful to have a few such ideas in your own armory. A good example is something a colleague of mine did some years ago.

The idea

From a management consultancy and training company . . .

This idea shows how something about a specific customer, in this case something that was almost chanced across, can be turned to advantage in a way that surprises. A consultant was visiting the Swedish manufacturer SKF in Gothenburg. At the company's ultra-modern office and factory there was a procedure used to impress visiting customers. They signed in, went about their business, then when they left they were presented with a smartly printed card, listing the time at which they had arrived, and that at which they were departing. Below this was a note of the precise number of ball bearings (the company's main product at the time) that had been produced in the factory during their visit. Even for a brief visit it was an impressive figure, and often it was in the millions. It made a nice public relations touch.

This consultant saw this for the first time after a visit in which he had discussed sales training with the marketing director. He asked the receptionist for an envelope, wrote the marketing director's name on it, and then wrote on the card, "But how many have you sold?" He asked for it to be sent up to the offices. When he won work with the company, he and his colleagues who were involved on the project were constantly asked, "Are you the guys who dared to send back the manufacturing count?" The gesture was impressive, the word went round, and it did their profile no harm at all. I have always wondered how important it was in actually winning the business. No matter, it cannot have done any harm, and it certainly had style.

In practice

- Be observant and think on your feet, always watching for opportunities.

- Consider carefully any idea that "pops up" like this for a moment as they will not all be viable.

29 ❓ THINK OF A NUMBER

SALESPEOPLE NEED MANY skills, not simply because selling is itself a complex process, but also because it must often work in conjunction with other skills such as negotiation. A prime one is numeracy. It is one that no salesperson can afford to neglect. I once heard of a salesperson having rings run around him by a buyer who kept tapping things out on a desktop calculator and making financial statements that were hard to rebut. He then discovered it was pure bluff—the machine was not switched on!

The idea

A story told at Henley Management College (and originally recounted in my book *Hook Your Audience*, published by Management Pocketbooks) . . .

A delegate on a management program at this renowned college by the River Thames could not get anything right regarding finance. By the time the course concluded, he was very much the class dunce. As attendees dispersed back to their respective companies the group agreed to meet up a year later to see how everyone was faring, and in due course a dinner was arranged at a smart restaurant. The "dunce" arrived a little late, but as he did so it was clear to all from the Porsche he parked outside, the suit he wore, and a dozen other signs of affluence, that he was doing very well for himself.

"I would never have thought it possible," said the course tutor. "Tell us, what are you doing?"

"It wasn't easy," he replied. "I was made redundant soon after the course finished. I then tried various things without much success, so I finally started up in business myself—in the import/export business in Africa. I discovered that I could buy things for $2 on one side of the border and sell them for $4 on the other. It's gone well—I'm still amazed at how that 2 percent adds up."

Digressing into financial techniques is beyond my remit here. Suffice to say that this is an area that some readers may feel it prudent to explore further. Instinct may not make up for a lack of understanding, as it did in the tale above! It is always annoying to lose a sale, all the more so if you know that the ability to come up with the right calculation quickly enough would have saved the day.

In practice

- Consider what things you might need to work out in advance of a meeting so that you can produce figures apparently without effort.

- If you are not sure, never plow on hoping it will be all right. Always check your costings, and if necessary say you need to do so. Get out the calculator and get it right!

LET ONE CUSTOMER SELL TO ANOTHER

SOMETIMES IN SELLING you will face situations and objections that seem intractable, ones that need outside evidence to overcome. There's no surprise there, you might say: aren't many of the things that provide proof or evidence to enhance credibility external factors? They certainly are, and a motoring magazine's road test of a car, or independent petrol consumption figures, are just cases in point.

Testimonials are common too, and act to beef up many a brochure as well as sales pitches.

The idea

From a sales training movie . . .

This idea is from a fictitious company. It is represented in what must be one of very few training movies aimed at sales managers, and dealing with an aspect of how to manage a team of salespeople. (The film, titled *Training Salesmen on the Job*, was made by Rank and distributed by Longman Training.)

In the movie we see a salesperson having difficulty with an objection. He is selling industrial equipment of some sort, and any company purchasing it must invest time and money in staff training to make sure that people can operate it effectively and safely. The buyer is interested, but is blocking, using the fact that a competitor offers training that can be done in significantly less time (thus reducing downtime and the cost of having operators away from their normal duties).

The salesperson tries to make the point that the extra investment is worthwhile, but the buyer is not convinced. The salesperson can clearly see that something more is necessary. Rather than offer vague testimonials and quote experience from elsewhere, he suggests that the prospect consult a particular and recent buyer. He clearly has the name researched and ready: it's one his prospect might even know. "Why don't you give him a ring?" he says. "I'm sure his experience will verify what I'm saying." He leaves the buyer to make the call. The fact that he's so open about it seems to make it likely that the call will be made. This is a very precise and upfront use of the testimonial, and one worth a thought.

In practice

- Again, this demands some thought and planning so that you can draw on a list of names as appropriate.

- Match people sensibly. For example don't suggest a huge company as a reference for a smaller one, or vice versa. You need people to believe the opinion they get will be relevant to their circumstances.

WORK AROUND INHERENT PROBLEMS

SOMETIMES THERE ARE problems that you know make selling more difficult, yet by their nature they are seemingly impossible to change. This example, where the hindrance is a physical fact, is taken from one particular industry. Because of the specific circumstances the solution is not one that would be necessary or possible for everyone, but like so many of the ideas here it demonstrates a kind of creative thinking that I applaud, and that you can imitate.

The idea

At a local distributor for Rank Xerox . . .

A certain office equipment distributor had an office and showroom in a medium-sized town (say the size of Cambridge in Britain). It was on a prime site but there was one drawback: there was no easy customer parking nearby, and none that was free. The few staff parking spaces were shared with the other businesses in the block in which it occupied the first floor. The company knew that many customers would not buy without a demonstration, and also surmised that the lack of parking put some people off from making a visit. Of course there were a number of things that might have helped, including moving the showroom, and banning the staff from parking on the premises so the spaces could be used for customers instead. One idea worked well, however.

The showroom was open on Saturdays, a day when staff in the offices above did not work. Following an idea generated by one of the team, the company did a deal with its neighbors to use their parking spaces on Saturdays. It then suggested in promotions and telephone prospecting calls that customers might come to a demonstration on a Saturday. This worked well. It soon discovered that for some male customers the attraction was free parking and an excuse to avoid shopping with their partner or family! This change extended the number of demonstrations given and thus saw sales rise.

In practice

- Are there things to do with your sales situation that might be exploited or changed to help your sales? Check.

BE AFRAID, BE VERY AFRAID

ONE TECHNIQUE THAT is essential to salespeople is closing. You can do everything else right, but closing badly or failing to close can scupper all the good work that has been put in. So no apologies for including a couple of good closes here. The first one was used on me by a small travel agent on faraway New Zealand's North Island.

The idea

From a New Zealand travel agent . . .

I travel regularly for work and holidays (indeed the first proposal for this book was written at 30,000 feet). So I deal regularly with travel agents, and I am often not particularly impressed. Should I have to spell out where Seoul is, for goodness sake? Sorry, I digress.

Anyway I was in touch with a firm in Auckland, since I had discovered that it was likely to be cheaper to book a trip onward from there than to do so from Britain. Because it was a long way to travel, and the project was cost-sensitive, I made the original inquiry well ahead of the time I expected to be traveling. I got a quote and acknowledged it, saying "decision later." Thereafter I got a series of reminders by email. These used the classic fear close: in this case a plea to book early, as the time at which I intended to travel was "peak season."

So far so normal, but what I felt made the follow-up contacts unusual was that they continued other parts of the sales pitch, and enhanced them too. The staff didn't just add a couple of lines saying hi: they took some time to refer to sights to be seen and things to be done, to mention particular places to go and to stay. Their chatty nature began to make me feel there was a relationship being built, and the chances of my using them increased steadily over some months. The frequency was not overdone, and it will be interesting to see what happens next if I leave the decision much longer. So far, so well done.

In practice

- This is both a nice variant on a classic method of closing, and a good example of persistence—surely an inherent characteristic of good salespeople.

- Making follow-up contacts interesting and thus more likely to be retained and acted upon is always going to work better than a routine "Anything I can do?" call.

MAKING ADMINISTRATION ASSIST SALES

SALESPEOPLE ARE NOT renowned for their love of administration (many don't apologize for this, just insisting that they have other qualities). Nevertheless it has to be done, and most salespeople have to complete call and order reports and more, though some systems are easier and quicker to complete than in the past, and many are now filed on screen and submitted as emails. One system that is vital, and that can make a significant contribution to sales effectiveness, is customer records.

There were always customer record cards in years gone by, but again many are now only accessed on a computer screen. The first point to make is that every salesperson should accept that these are company records and not personal ones. Of course you use them and they must help you, but you may move on or have an accident and be unable to work. At such a time the company expects that you will have been keeping records in such a way that not only will someone else be able to pick them up and understand them, but also they will contain sufficient information for someone else to operate from. Sadly this is not always the case. How are yours? Be honest.

Of course, reference to record cards should help pick up the threads of past conversations with customers in a way that helps prepare the right kind of call and run the right kind of meeting next time. But records can also contain information that assists sales productivity, and that is less usual.

The idea

From Oxford University Press . . .

A new member of the team of sales representatives at this academic and general publisher once told me something of the induction process. The rep was to visit both bookshops and academic establishments such as schools and universities, and was taking over from another person who had been promoted. The records were clear and up to date, and they went further than expected. Do you know, she told me, that there were specific suggestions and directions for where to park for every single customer! Anyone who has tried to park in the labyrinthine maze of many a university campus will recognize how useful and time-saving that must have been. Indeed given the number of accounts involved it must have helped the compiler almost as much as it helped the newcomer. I bet it saw more calls made and more books sold.

In practice

- Remember records are corporate, not personal.

- Thoroughness here may save time, and allow more pointed action to be taken by you and others.

THE USEFULNESS OF "GATEKEEPERS"

"THE BUYER" MAY be a person, but it may be more than one person: several working together in some way, the board of directors, or a committee. In any case this or these are probably not the only people that a salesperson meets in the course of dealing with a customer. Others include receptionists, secretaries, assistants, and whoever brings you a cup of tea, if you are welcomed hospitably. More senior people can be involved too. First consider the nature of the gatekeeper description. Gatekeepers are people who can allow or deny access to others, ultimately the decision maker. So a sensible rule here is to never, ever get on the wrong side of someone in that position. Beyond that, though, can you actively canvass their help?

Sometimes the relationships are such that you can draw people in. Saying to one person, "What does Mary think about it?" might bring a response to the effect that they are not involved, but it might prompt a new thought, especially if you have offered a reason that their opinion might help. "Mary has a lot of customer contact, doesn't she? What's her view?" Even bring the other person into the discussion on an ongoing basis. Even where there is no apparent link, people other than the buyer can be useful.

The idea

Allied Carpets: the chatty salesperson . . .

George works selling carpets. Many customers come to the store, and other inquiries start with a meeting elsewhere: in a company office, say. George has a rule. When he sits in someone's reception he chats to the receptionist. "What's it like working here?" is a favorite lead-in, and receptionists as a breed are sufficiently put upon to often want to talk. Regularly such conversations lead to additional sales. Perhaps George says he is there to, say, do a quote for the boardroom, but he's told, "But it's the showroom that could really do with a new carpet. You should see the state of it in there." He can sometimes even persuade the receptionist to give him a sight of such a place. Then it is an easy matter to introduce it into a conversation with a buyer, and (economies of scale work well here, he says) often he obtains an additional sale. Maybe he gets a date or two with the receptionist as well.

In practice

- Many people you come across in a customer's organization may be able to assist you to sell.

- Even one small piece of information can be helpful.

- Explore all such contacts (carefully).

35 CHECK, CHECK, AND CHECK AGAIN

THERE IS SOMETHING about putting things into writing that, for many people, dilutes their communication. It's just not everyone's forte, at least without some thought. Many salespeople see writing the written proposals that are a necessary part of the sales process in a good many businesses as a chore. (And if you think a proposal is a bit of a job, try a book!) Regarding it as a chore tends to make things worse, as it can lead to rushed and scrappy writing. Cutting and pasting standard documents is a hazard too: I received one recently that suddenly referred to me as Margaret halfway through.

Yet these documents are vital and need to be write (sic). There is a hotel in Britain that was reported as having a sign inside all its bedroom doors that read, "In the interests of security please ensure that your bedroom door is firmly closed before entering or leaving your room." Someone wrote that, printed it, and stuck it on hundreds of doors, and still no one noticed it is rubbish; and that is just one short sentence.

Linguistic nonsenses, and spelling mistakes too, really matter. (Spell-checkers do not catch everything, especially customer names, and I know of someone who lost potential business because the organization Express Dairies was written as "Express Diaries" on the title page of a proposal.) In such circumstances customers will often think, "What else don't they bother about?" Especially when service is an important consideration, they are entitled so to do. So care is always necessary—and here is an idea that helps.

The idea

This is done in a number of organizations . . .

Curiously perhaps, among the organizations doing this are the kind where you might expect writing skills to be reasonably high. For instance, I know more than one large law firm where this is the case, and the same is true of accountants.

The idea is simply stated: there is a mandatory rule that no written sales proposal is allowed to be sent until it has been read over by someone other than its writer. It may sound draconian, but if it prevents the loss of one significant order it is worthwhile. If it is done on a swap basis between colleagues, the time taken is kept manageable and fairly allocated.

In practice

- This may need review and policy setting.

- If there are rules, follow them, as the example above shows it is all too easy for (avoidable) mistakes to do damage.

36

MIX BUSINESS AND CHAT APPROPRIATELY

Given the emphasis placed on customer relationships these days (yet another set of initials entered the language a while ago—CRM, customer relationship management—and there are more variants), it is not surprising that all salespeople try to get along with their customers. Sometimes the social element is very important, and sometimes people genuinely become friends. Often though, a good business relationship with a measure of friendly interaction is what is called for. "Called for" is, I think, the right phrase: a good customer relationship is what the customer wants and finds useful.

Finding the right mix can be difficult. I make no apologies for the following being an apocryphal story, as it makes a good point. A salesperson is asked how she manages to do such good business with a particular customer. She mentions various things: the appropriateness of the product, the right level of service, but finishes by saying, "A key thing is that I discovered a while back that John's a golf fanatic. As long as I remember to ask all about his game, how he's done in competitions, and so on, the relationship stays fine."

Then the buyer is asked why he gives so much business to this supplier. He too talks about the product, the service, and how he finds the salesperson a good and efficient contact, but he finishes by saying, "I'm a busy man, I do rather wish she didn't waste so much time talking about my golf."

The idea

Just a thought from this story . . .

It really is difficult to rule a line here with certainty. As the story shows, it is easy to misread the situation, especially as most people are essentially polite. The moral is clear: this should not be an area that just "sort of develops."

In practice

- Make a point of thinking about and perhaps asking about what is appropriate (perhaps simply under the guise of checking how much time pressure someone is under).

- And you need to check occasionally that the prevailing practice of the moment continues to be appropriate for the buyer.

- Finally: if in doubt, use less chat rather than more.

NOW YOU'RE MOTORING

For many a field salesperson the ubiquitous company car (which for the most part the inherent unfairness of life dictates is never really what you want) is a major part of their life and equipment. How often does a customer ride in your car? How often do they see inside it, as they walk you out to the parking area perhaps? And what do they think of it if they do? Does it enhance your image of efficiency, or does it position you as the ultimate slob?

Last time I went in a salesperson's car it took a full five minutes to clear a space for me. What needed to be moved was not primarily business material, rather it was the detritus of what was clearly a hectic personal life. There was a baby seat in the back, toys, empty crisp packets and a banana peel on the floor, and this was clearly the one place in our regulated world in which the rep was permitted to smoke. Urgh!

This kind of mess is unlikely to give the right impression. I don't mind the baby seat, but surely an effort should be made to keep a car clean and reasonably tidy. On the other hand there are hazards at the other end of the scale. I treasure the moment when I asked a prospect of mine whether they were talking to any other firms (a useful question, let me say in passing), and was told, "Yes, but as the first guy who came to see me arrived in a Porsche, I felt I should get another quote." I leave you to judge whether my getting the business, but not driving a Porsche myself, rates as success or failure.

The idea

Dealing with the Ford Motor Company . . .

Another example: I know of another firm doing work for a major car manufacturer that hires its cars especially so that its people can turn up in something "appropriate," because there are none made by the customer in its fleet. If needs must.

In practice

- A car does not just get you from A to B. Think about how it contributes to your image, and make sure it does so in a positive way.

38 VOLUME, VOLUME, VOLUME

THE SIMPLEST FORM of selling is just asking a question. Perhaps it is not strictly a selling technique, but it can have a persuasive effect. Imagine you are going out for a meal. The barman who says, "A double?" or "Another drink, sir?" is selling, as is the waiter who asks, "Would you like a dessert?" (It's better still if they hand you a menu or ask you having already wheeled the dessert trolley to your elbow, as willpower withers more easily when you see what's available. That often gets an order that might not otherwise have been received.) This sort of thing does not need training or technique, it just needs to be remembered and applied on every occasion.

It is worth nailing this thought to a specific firm, and the example that follows makes some additional points.

The idea

The "telephone bank" First Direct . . .

First Direct is the telephone (and now internet) arm of HSBC. From its inception it has had a high reputation for service. The system works like this: you ring up, someone answers, you ask for some information or for something to be done, and it is done. All this is done not just politely, but also with real feeling. You may talk to someone different each time, but they still manage to make you feel you have a relationship with them; indeed, you do. In addition, there is no struggling to make out a voice coming to you from the other side of the world in an unfathomable accent. Many of the staff are in

Scotland (and so they all pronounce my name correctly!). You will gather I bank with First Direct and like the company.

Its staff do sell to me: savings accounts, traveler's checks, holiday insurance, and more are all mentioned at one time or another. But— and this is important to what is essentially a service operation— they do not overdo it. Such things are not mentioned too often, and they do not go into a strident sulking bleat if you do not express interest, as so many people selling on the telephone do. It is all done courteously, and never seems to dilute the good image they project. Yet I am sure it pays dividends: the volume of calls the call centers handle is prodigious.

In practice

- The moral here is that when you discover a good, simple idea that works for you and is accepted by your customers, use it a lot.

- Selling is a numbers game in more ways than one.

LINE UP THE WHOLE TEAM BEHIND THE SALESPERSON

I ONCE TELEPHONED the office of a salesperson I dealt with regularly for a while (in a plastics company from which I bought ring binders to use on training courses). Since he was usually out "on the road," I did not expect to find him in except by chance. I asked the switchboard operator for him by name and without comment, and was told, "I'm afraid he's rarely in the office during the day. He's only a salesperson." *Only* a salesperson? This was a guy who had spent time telling me that he was the most important contact I could have in his organization, and for all I knew his image was being regularly sabotaged by such remarks on a daily basis.

If you wonder why this occurs, consider: there can be something of a them and us situation between inside staff and field sales staff. Largely, in my view, this is because the sales role is not understood. The prevailing image is of people able to swan about in their smart company cars all day with very little supervision. If the sales side is misunderstood, then the sales side must do something about it. Support staff and what they do are intimately connected with sales activity. If the salesperson asks someone to send samples, for example, and they are late going out, then it is the salesperson who gets the customer moaning at them. It's tempting to lay blame—it's those idiots in dispatch again—but this does not really help the customer.

The idea

From a plastics binder company . . .

I told my plastics binders contact about my experience, and he was incensed. He led a campaign to educate a variety of people around his organization, getting permission for people from the switchboard, dispatch, the accounts department, and so on to spend time with him out visiting customers. Most were instantly more appreciative of the job the field sales team did, and cooperation and collaboration increased markedly as a result; so too did overall customer service. Such action could be described as a short, sharp shock to the people involved. Its effect would need reinforcing later on, but that too is worthwhile.

In practice

- Consider who you might educate about your sales role, and what difference might it make to service and to your sales results.

- Make this a regular job, briefing new appointees as they arrive.

SELL IN COLLABORATION WITH SOMEONE ELSE

SOMETIMES THERE ARE significant problems in selling. One such is when the status quo is powerful. Customers are using something else that they find satisfactory, and it blinds them to the possibility that you are offering something different and better. However good a salesperson you are, you may conclude that a sufficient degree of credibility can only come from cooperation with someone else.

The idea

A personal initiative from the vice chair of Sony USA . . .

A dramatic example of the principle involved here occurred when technology in the music business first moved away from vinyl records with the invention of CDs. Record companies were wedded to the existing technology, and were intent on avoiding change and protecting their present investment in it. Given this block, the answer for those promoting CDs was to take a step back and ask, who is likely to be most interested in a new medium that improves the quality of recorded sound? The answer was the recording artists themselves—the music makers. They gave initial demonstrations to this group, with predictable results: the technology really was better, and they loved it.

Subsequently approaches to the industry, backed by this feedback, persuaded the record company executives first to take a real look at what was being offered, then to adopt it. Not only did sales of recorded music switch quite quickly to CDs; huge sales resulted as people bought second copies of music they already owned in the new format.

In practice

- There are many possibilities here. Ask yourself, who could augment your sales pitch? Customers, outside experts, other staff in your own organization (technical people, perhaps)—all may have something to contribute if you can harness their contribution and support.

TELL PEOPLE YOU'VE WON AN AWARD

Given that any salesperson needs to build a case, and that one huge reason to buy is not normally going to persuade everyone, you need to seek out a number of factors that together combine to produce a weight of a case that is irresistible. Your product may only have a certain number of benefits, and it is difficult to create more (certainly without changing the product), but credibility factors are another matter. Not only may there be many things to add here; you may be able to take action to ensure that there are more.

The idea

Lonely Planet travel guides . . .

These guides are now well known and successful, but their start was not meteoric and at one time their future hung in the balance. The *Lonely Planet Guide to India* won the prestigious Thomas Cook Travel Guidebook Award. This might be called lucky, but the company did of course have to ensure that the book was good, and enter it so that it was considered for the award. One of the founders of the company, Tony Wheeler, was quoted as saying, "It took us to another level. It really opened doors and made a huge difference for us." He was saying more than that the award was announced on the cover of the book: he was surely saying it was how the company used the fact that made the difference. You can imagine the enthusiasm with which the representatives of a comparatively new and small company included this fact in their sales presentation at that time.

Of course your product most likely is no contender for this award, but the amount of awards to be won is legion. A product and a sales pitch can benefit from anything, from the firm's founder being "business person of the year" to awards for technical excellence, quality, staff, customer service, and more. Many such awards are on an industry basis, while others are national, or local to a town or county.

In practice

- Find out what awards are open to your product or service, and how to go after them. (Suggest an application to management if it needs support.) A winning story can add to a winning case and enhance the sales presentations you make.

MAKE PEOPLE BELIEVE YOU ARE SUCCESSFUL

THIS HEADING SHOULD perhaps be followed by the words, "even when you are not." There is no question that success, however you may choose to define it, is a sign—one that lends conviction to a sales argument. If you are successful, people will figure that you must have customers, and they must be happy customers too or you would soon cease to be successful. Conversely if you are not (yet) successful it is difficult to get a hearing; and this makes it difficult for companies, and salespeople, in their early days.

The idea

Jerry Della Femina throws a party . . .

Jerry Della Femina is a heavyweight of the American advertising business, but it was not always thus. One advertising agency he started was slow to attract clients, and it looked as if it might well founder. As Christmas approached he decided to pour his last remaining funds into an epic Christmas party. He sent more than a thousand invitations to journalists and potential clients, and put on "one hell of a do."

People love to be associated with success. The "big do" indicated success, and a large number of those invited attended. It gave him and his colleagues an opportunity to sell to them, and do so in a positive atmosphere. Instead of questions being asked, assumptions were made about the success and substance of the operation. Meetings were set up, deals were done, and as January got under way new clients were signed up. A snowball effect had been created, literally in one (expensive!) evening.

Sometimes an extravagant gesture needs to be part of selling, or, as here, to lead into it. This tactic did two things: it produced face-to-face contact with key potential clients (and engendered some public relations coverage from doing so), and also created an image of success that changed the nature of subsequent sales conversations. And, by all accounts, it was a great party.

In practice

- Think carefully before doing this sort of thing. In the example above the financial risk was considerable.

- Such things work best when they combine a display of success with additional opportunities to sell.

SHOW PEOPLE YOUR SIZE

Size is an important measure contributing to the overall image of an organization. If the entire operation consists of one man and a (small) dog, it is difficult to give the impression of a multinational conglomerate, at least without telling some significant untruths. Certainly successful selling may necessitate some serious exaggeration, but you may draw the line at telling a straight lie, if only on the basis of the risk of being caught out. On the other hand you may be able to be strictly honest and yet give the impression that your company is grander than it really is.

The idea

From BigStar, an online video and DVD retailer . . .

Wanting people to think of it as a major player, this company budgeted for some advertising. Its logo appeared on several hundred trucks in key regions of its market (New York, Los Angeles, and more). The logo was presented in a way that made the trucks look like BigStar's own vehicles, although in fact it had no delivery fleet, and all deliveries were contracted out. Customer awareness increased substantially, and sales staff stopped having to talk up the company's size and status, because people simply saw it as large.

Another example of this comes from a small British company. It was pitching for business with a large organization: success would take it up the scale and into a bigger league. The company knew who would be at the presentation it would make, and sent several members of staff to follow some of these key people home. They found that they all commuted by rail into London. The next move was to book some posters at the stations these decision makers used. With a limited budget, the company booked them nowhere else and only had them put up for the couple of weeks ahead of the presentation. At the presentation, when the staff were describing the company's operations and activity, they mentioned casually, "You may have seen our current poster campaign." The audience nodded. They got the business.

In practice

- You may feel these tactics are contrived, or deceptive even, but certainly they are both creative solutions. They are examples of action specifically taken, and linked to in sales meetings, that achieves a well-thought-out purpose and impresses customers.

- Even a small measure of this principle can be useful and add to your credibility.

SURPRISE THEM WITH YOUR WRITING

THE WRITTEN WORD is not everyone's strong suit in terms of communication. Salespeople often feel more comfortable in a face-to-face situation, and feel most confident of it too. Faced with having to put something into writing, they can produce something turgid, replete with gobbledegook and "businessspeak," that is so over-formal and impersonal that it serves only to alienate people. "Who is this person?" the readers ask themselves. But it is possible for something unexpected and well conceived to create real impact, more so if it stands out from the banality sent by others.

The idea

From my own past . . .

This example is from the last stages of the sale, where things can so often stick at a "Leave it with me" stage. It makes the point that sometimes there is little new left to say. You can only repeat "It's me again," especially if you reckon the proposition is good and the only reason for lack of confirmation is timing or distraction, rather than the customer being totally unconvinced. Then the job is to continue to maintain contact, and ultimately to jog people into action, while appearing distinctive or memorable in the process.

After I had written a short book for a specialist publisher, I was keen to write another for it, on a different topic but in the same format. I proposed the idea, and got a generally good reaction—but no confirmation. I wrote and telephoned numerous times. Nothing: just a delay or a put-off (you may know the feeling!). Finally, when a prompt to chase came up yet again in my diary, I felt I had exhausted all the conventional possibilities. I sat down and wrote the following:

> Struggling author, patient, reliable (non-smoker), seeks commission on business topics. Novel formats preferred, but anything considered within reason; ideally 100 or so pages, on a topic like sales excellence sounds good—maybe with some illustrations. Delivery of the right quantity of material—on time—guaranteed. Contact me at the above address/telephone number or meet on neutral ground, carrying a copy of *Publishing News* and wearing a carnation.

I must confess I hesitated over it a little, thinking it perhaps too informal (I was sending it to someone I had met only once), but I signed and posted it. Gratifyingly, I got confirmation of my contract the following day (and you can read the result, *The Sales Excellence Pocketbook*, published by Management Pocketbooks).

In practice

- Sometimes a slightly less conventional approach works well. You should not reject anything other than the conventional approach; try a little experiment and see what it can do for you.

- Because prevailing standards are often low, this can be an easy area in which to "shine" (provided you act with care).

ASK FOR REFERRALS

SOMETIMES WE ARE reluctant to ask for referrals, yet if you are recommended to a prospect by someone who already buys from you (and is satisfied), that's likely to give you a small head start. So why is there a reluctance to ask? Is it embarrassment perhaps, or fear of rejection or failure? It is not likely that an existing and happy customer (obviously don't ask any dissatisfied ones!) will be angry or upset at your asking. They might see it as inappropriate in some way, but if so they are most likely to decline politely, not shout at you.

The idea

Many people do this, but I'll credit my thinking of it here to the guy who drives me to the airport . . .

Steve runs a taxi company. Actually that description does his operation a disservice: he runs a "luxury car service," and specializes in weddings and events, runs to the airport and longer journeys. He charges just a little bit more than the Mondeo cowboys who frequent the various taxi companies in the town. (Actually I must not malign them all, but some are perhaps just a touch unreliable.) Steve always turns up on time, wears a suit, and drives a rather nice Mercedes. In the car are newspapers, something to drink, and interesting conversation if you want it. On the customer service front you cannot find anything to criticize, and that is always a good foundation for selling.

Steve has learned that referral is a good way to build a business, and always asks if there is anyone he can contact or to whom you can pass on his details. The business card he hands over alongside this request is of good quality, and he can provide a more detailed postcard-sized information card too (which mentions for example that he has a six-seater vehicle as well as regular cars). This is the sort of idea that is so simple, so routine, and yet often neglected. Steve makes it a priority, and each time I book to travel with him he seems to be busier. See you on the 22nd, Steve.

In practice

- First, if you do this kind of thing you need to support it with the right material.

- Then it needs to be made a firm habit.

46 REMOVE FEAR OF RISK

MANY BUYERS ARE fearful of the decision you ask them to take. They feel insecure, they lack knowledge, they lack experience, they are conscious of acting for others—what will my boss say?—and all these feelings and more amount to the same thing: they are fearful of failure. They worry about the consequences if the product does not work, does not perform as expected, or any sort of shortfall appears after purchase. The good salesperson is aware of this, and sets out to diminish this fear during a sales meeting. But is there more you can do?

The idea

When Phoebe was six years old . . .

She wanted a kitten. This reminds me of a remark I saw on the internet, attributed to Annabel (also aged six): if you want a guinea pig, start by asking for a pony. Never have I come across a clearer indication of the nature of negotiation: ten more years and she will be a force to be reckoned with. Sorry, I digress. Imagine that Phoebe's parents went through the first stage and agreed to her having the kitten. They checked out various sources, and soon found that this was a difficult purchase. What was the right time for a kitten to leave its parents? Had it been inoculated, was it healthy? The last thing they wanted was for Phoebe to be upset by her new kitten falling sick, or, worse, dying.

One breeder suggested that they choose a kitten and take it home. (He threw in some free food for the first few weeks.) Then he would contact them in four weeks' time to check that the kitten was fit and well. Only at that stage would they pay for the kitten, and any signs of trouble would mean they could choose a new one. It was not a guarantee (the kitten might still be sick), but it displayed great confidence. If he could make that kind of offer, it was unlikely that he had not really inoculated the little cat.

In practice

- Consider not just diminishing the risk, but reversing it (as above). Here it means the risk is with the breeder, not the customer. That's attractive.

- See if you can find ways of reversing any risk your customers may feel they are being asked to take. If you can, they will like it.

TAKE YOUR TIME

MANY PRODUCTS AND services are non-standard. A kitchen can be designed and tailored to fit your needs and your house, a landscape gardener works in a similar way, many computer systems and consultancy of all sorts are bespoke. To a degree this is one of the strengths of such products, and one of the things that persuades the customer and prompts purchase.

But there is a danger. If the customer does not believe the product or service is really bespoke (when that is what they want), but suspects what they are being offered is actually just a standard option, then a unique aspect of it is negated and selling becomes that much more difficult. Even if there is a "good fit," they may believe they are being short-changed; certainly perception of price may well change.

The idea

This is a common problem in consultancy, which is part of my own work portfolio . . .

There are two stages to making bespoke suggestions. The first is identifying the individual circumstances, the second making a specific suggestion based on observation and some sort of survey. Often the second involves a written proposal. For example: the kitchen supplier must draw up and submit drawings and costs, and the consultant must propose how work will be carried out and write a detailed proposal. In both cases the instinct in terms of customer service is to jump to it and do this promptly.

The idea here is simple: take your time.

In practice

- Of course, you must check how urgently the proposal is needed, and make sure what you do will be satisfactory to the customer, but the time taken will be seen as in direct relationship to the degree of tailoring involved. If the proposal is based on a thorough survey, well described and presented, and delivered some time after the survey (even if it only takes a moment to customize it), the customer will assume it to be truly bespoke. It will be seen as having higher value than a standard offering.

- Allow sufficient time to show that some thought has gone into them, and your proposals may be valued more highly.

48 PUT OVER A CONSISTENT MESSAGE

Customers find it offputting to check something out and find that different parts of an organization give even slightly different messages, yet especially with complex products it can be difficult to get everyone singing from the same hymn sheet. Product knowledge is mentioned more than once in these pages, and having the right information in the right form is vital if selling is going to be successful. Prospects find it more difficult to understand the complexities of a proposal if they hear slightly different things from different people.

The idea

From global telecoms company Cable & Wireless . . .

Cable & Wireless operates in more than 70 countries. One regional division has activities especially well spread, with operations current in markets as diverse and far-flung as the Solomon Islands and the West Indies. When it launched a range of new internet products there was a need to ensure that members of the widely dispersed sales team understood them sufficiently well to do justice to selling them, and indeed to get the launch off to a good start.

The team was given the information through specially designed e-learning, which addressed the basic technical knowledge that salespeople needed, together with the benefits and how to put them over to customers. The approach was designed to be lively and visual (for example equating networks to traffic and motorway junctions). After a pilot, the scheme was made available simultaneously to some 1,400 staff, 94 percent of whom reported favorably on both method and content.

In practice

Several points seem inherent here:

- First, the company rated the importance of product knowledge highly.

- Second, this approach assisted the product launch to a considerable extent. It might have been a slower and less certain process if trainer(s) had had to travel the world conducting endless courses. The steps that were taken to ensure everyone involved had an excellence of knowledge from the moment of the launch paid dividends.

- The wise salesperson pays attention to any assistance of this sort.

SPEAK THEIR LANGUAGE

THIS SECTION ACKNOWLEDGES that not all selling takes place in the home country of the salesperson doing it. Some operations are multinational, and whatever the first language of their employees, many such companies have English as their "business language." However, if you are to create sufficient rapport with your overseas customers you may need to do more than simply speak to them in business English.

The idea

From website management company Attenda . . .

Attenda can provide its service to clients around the world from offices in Britain, and has multilingual staff available 24 hours a day. However, research showed that potential clients in Germany wanted to deal with a local company, and with German people. David Godwin, vice president, reckoned, "We are not big enough to buck the system," so the company set up a German subsidiary. The people selling Attenda's service there are German employees of what is positioned as a local company. Whatever other problems they may have in a competitive field, no cross-cultural problems should hamper their sales success.

Similarly, Printronic International, Europe's leading data-processing computer bureau, also has strong language capabilities. Its manaaging director says, "despite English being the global business language our experiences in Europe still point to national languages being the preferred choice [of our customers]." As always, it would seem that selling—in this case quite technical services—is dependent on clarity of explanation, and dealing with clients in the way they want to be dealt with.

In practice

- Whether what is needed is just a few polite words at the start of a meeting, or the conduct of the whole sales process, if it is done in the language of the customer it is sure to be appreciated.

- There is obviously some effort involved here, but there should be a worthwhile payoff. Your business circumstance will dictate what you need to do.

MAKE DESCRIPTION RING A BELL

THERE CAN BE a problem in describing even the best product in terms that make sense to the customer. This problem is worsened if the product is new and unknown. The advice to salespeople is always to be truly descriptive, but in these circumstances it's easy to become vague and include the words "sort of" early on. Customers tend to be defeated by this. The trick is to find the right way to explain what the product is like, and that starts with the customer.

The idea

From the out-of-this-world world of *Star Trek* . . .

The television series *Star Trek* is now a legend across the globe. The original series may have started slowly, but it gained cult status, spawned several spinoffs across many years, and led to a series of successful movies. Financially it became one of the most successful such franchises ever, so perhaps it is difficult now to remember how different it was at its inception from other programs being broadcast at the time. Creator Gene Roddenberry had to find a way of pitching his program idea to the networks. He thought he had a truly novel idea, yet he knew that those he sought to persuade were conservative, and that many of the programs they accepted were close to something already existing—the classic known quantity.

One of the most successful series at the time was *Wagon Train*. That was set in the American West, but the plot and the characters were essentially similar to Roddenberry's idea for a space odyssey. Each episode involved the same tight-knit group moving on to pastures new, and dealt with what happened to them in the new location, and the people they met there. Roddenberry sold *Star Trek* by describing it as *Wagon Train* in space. At the time this was a well-chosen analogy. The programmers understood it, and despite the risk of something so new and different, he got agreement to make the program. The rest, as they say, is history.

In practice

- Just one idea and one key description can create the distinction that is required for sales success.

- Often this is best done not by thinking of how you think your product or service is special, but by finding a good comparison that makes sense to the customer. So boldly go . . .

SURPRISE CUSTOMERS WITH SPEED OF RESPONSE

A RAPID RESPONSE used to mean a brochure sent out on the day that a request for one arrived. Now communications are different: we email and text instantly, and can look at company details in real time on the internet. At the same time technology can slow things down and annoy people. For example, who has not had a bad experience with automated telephone systems? We ring . . . and we wait. We go through interminable selection of options (which always seem to put "Just let me speak to someone" at the end of a long list), and listen to music we detest, and endless statements that "Your call is important to us." Clearly little has been done to actually demonstrate that. I am getting on a hobbyhorse here, but it's still the case that it is wise not to do this, or anything like it. However, sometimes it is possible to use technology in a way that truly impresses, and provides genuinely good service.

The idea

From the subcontinent of India . . .

India is an enigma. It's a huge country, with millions of poor people, as well as a burgeoning economy, and everything it takes to be a major tourist attraction. Oberoi Hotels feature on the itinerary of many visitors wanting to do things in style. As with many hotels, many overseas customers now make first contact with them by looking at the website, through which you can also send a message asking for any specific information needed.

Recently when I did just that, I did not receive a message back over the ether. Instead I received a telephone call not much more than 15 minutes later from the company's British representative. Much of the time, the time difference between the countries makes it possible to do this in working hours, and it is impressive: a virtually instantaneous response from someone that you think of as being too far off for such action.

In practice

- The salesperson who responds promptly is in a strong position. They have all the details the customer has provided, they impress with a timely response, perhaps unexpectedly so, and are ideally placed to make the most of the contact.

- Ensure that internal organization promotes this sort of thing, and never allow systems and administration to hinder it (as so often happens).

KEEP CUSTOMERS THINKING OF YOU

IT IS HARDLY a new idea to keep in touch with customers. Memories are short, especially when people are busy, and exposed to numerous other messages from other people and organizations. So most salespeople do it to some degree or another, but sometimes it is regarded as a waste of time. For instance, the very nature of the business might make it inappropriate. Or does it?

The idea

From a specialist retailer . . .

When repeat purchases are a possibility, most businesses make an effort to stay in touch with customers. But when they are not, further contact can seem like a waste of time. Yet one company shows that this is not always true. It is a specialist retailer selling wedding dresses. The average marriage may not always last as long as it used to do, but even so a customer is hardly likely to come in a fortnight after their wedding wanting another wedding dress.

Yet this retailer scheduled in (and budgeted for) a number of specific follow-up contacts after the dress was delivered and paid for. It sent flowers and a card on the big day to wish the couple well, an invitation to a function a month or so later, a card on their anniversary—for several years. And more. Why take this line? Why spend money and effort in this way? Because people getting married are often at a stage in life when they know others in a similar position, and with something as memorable as a wedding, the likelihood of recommendation can be high. (Maybe 50 percent of customers in such a shop are there, in whole or part, through recommendation.) If the dress was a picture, if the day was memorable, then enhancing the idea of just how helpful the provider of the dress (and perhaps other elements of the wedding arrangements too) was is highly likely to increase the number of referrals. This idea is much more straightforward and cost-effective than canvassing more widely for new business. And those who come inquiring because a friend suggested it are that much easier to sell to than colder prospects.

In practice

- Whatever the time scale, ensure that this sort of follow-up and potential recommendation is possible in your business. Even if the traditional view does not make how to do it immediately obvious, it is worth some thought to find a way.

GUARANTEE AS MUCH AS YOU CAN

Any purchase puts the customer in the position of taking a risk. This is very clear with anything mechanical—the customer wonders whether it will go wrong, and if it does, how things will be handled and what it will cost in time and money. Given that customers have this worry, can you take advantage of it?

The idea

From the motor manufacturer Hyundai . . .

Cars are certainly a product for which people worry about reliability. A failed car can not only cost you time and money; it can leave you stranded, risking other things like your reputation at work, or ability to visit someone in hospital. So customers want a guarantee. Over the years the length of the guarantees offered has increased—a year, two years, more—and they do provide confidence and make a sale more likely.

As I write this, Hyundai is offering a full five-year guarantee, and certain aspects of the car are covered for longer than that. Given that this is not the most famous make of car, I suspect that this must help sales success significantly, not just because of the length of coverage but also because of what it implies about Hyundai's confidence in its products, and how it compares with some larger and better-known manufacturers. Five years is longer than many people keep a car, so the guarantee is likely to impress.

This is part of the risk-reversal process referred to elsewhere. The device is here being used as a major sales aid by making the time covered by the warranty extra-long, perhaps unexpectedly long.

In practice

- There is a principle here that can be used in many businesses where, because of their nature, customers worry about reliability and the consequences of something causing problems.

54 KEEP THEIR ATTENTION

It is bad enough when a customer's attention wanders. It is worse when you know—or realize later—that it is your fault it is happening. Sometimes when a customer's mind does wander, whatever is causing it has nothing to do with you; it was in train before you arrived. If you notice a lack of attention, it is worth pausing, and checking by asking, "Is this a bad moment?" If necessary—at worst—you may feel it is best to abandon the meeting and set a new time. I have done this several times, and always thought that time proved me right. In some cases it jumped client relations ahead positively because it was appreciated.

The idea

From those wonderful people at Microsoft . . .

The idea here addresses the problem of inattention highlighted above, and does so in a way that is very specific to computer presentations using PowerPoint. You might be in a one-on-one meeting, putting your laptop on the buyer's desk, or you might be giving a more formal presentation involving several, or many, people. PowerPoint presentations can be powerful, enabling you to use a series of images to enhance your point. (Remember that any slides you show should support your case, not lead it, and certainly not replace it.) Just because the technique is powerful it commands attention. So, when you originate a presentation, do not fill the screen with things that distract, and switch off the image when you want the customer to focus exclusively on you.

I am amazed how many people, when I suggest switching the screen off, say, "But how do I do that?" PowerPoint and Microsoft have made it easy: you simply press the "B" key (B for blank, if that helps you remember). The image fades, the screen goes dark, concentration and the customer's focus of attention return to you, and with another press of the "B" key you can resume on exactly the image you left. This is so useful; it puts you in more powerful control, and as a result increases the likelihood of sales success.

In practice

- Do not let your sales approach inadvertently distract the customer.

- Organize yourself in a way that gets them to focus on what you want throughout the meeting.

55 USE YOUR CUSTOMERS' TIMING

SOMETIMES IT IS difficult to know the best time to do something. This is true of anything in life: when should you apply for a new job, move to the country, or just broach the subject of what color the living room should be painted with your partner? With customers we always seem to have a sense of urgency. We not only want an order, we want it soon, or even right now. This may be understandable, but it reflects a focus on us, not on them.

Information is the key to choosing the right time. An early boss of mine once made a light-hearted comment to the effect that he had got himself a pay rise by saying it was a leap year and he had to work harder. I stored the remark away for two years until another leap year came along, then reminded him of it. I got a laugh and a small extra rise. With customers the information you glean and act on may be different, but the effect can be similar.

The idea

This from a company selling office furniture . . .

It is often helpful to customer relations if you involve yourself to some degree in your customers' lives. You need to think about whether it is useful to send them a Christmas card or something on their birthday, whether to mention a work-related anniversary you know about (maybe they have been at the organization for ten years, or it is 100 years since the business was started). It may be useful to note other things that come up in conversation too. It's nice to be able to ask at the next meeting, "How did your son do in that exam?" or "Did you have a good holiday in Crete?"

But one event in your customers' lives is key to sales success. It is the timing of their financial year and the budgeting that goes with it. Find out when this is (and perhaps something of how the budgeting process works), and it can help your timing very specifically. You can then consider: is a purchase best suggested ahead of the new year, to mop up funds in this year's budget, or once the new budget is in place? Mention your thinking, and you'll be seen as fitting your suggestions to the realities of your customer's situation, rather than just pushing for an order now.

In practice

- The starting point of all such things is questions. Do not forget to ask.

- Keep clear notes. Sometimes information may not prove useful for some weeks or months, but you want to remember and not waste the opportunity it presents.

GET THE COMPETITION INTO THE DISCUSSION

It is axiomatic that decrying the competition is not a good idea. If you say to a customer that company X is rubbish, it always turns out that the person deals with them, likes them, or their brother-in-law works for them. Rather than giving you an edge, it can easily be self-defeating: it makes you sound defensive, arrogant, or just plain spiteful. None are attractive characteristics, or likely to help create rapport or a good relationship. But dealing with the question of the competition may be unavoidable in a conversation.

The idea

From many a different industry . . .

If a customer brings a competitor into the conversation, especially if they ask your opinion of it—"How do you compare with X?"—the best tactic may be to praise your rival. Indeed it may well work best to lay it on with a trowel: "From what I hear the company has a good reputation, makes excellent products, and always seems to deliver on time." Such a statement may well prompt a response that pulls back a bit. "We've done some business with them, and they're fine," your customer might reply, "but I wouldn't go that far. We did have one delivery problem." This has brought you into a conversation that helps you position the customer's relationship with competitors and attitude to them, and this should make what comes next easier. Even if the customer agrees with you, the exchange might be useful. At the least, it might help you decide such a relationship is impossible to challenge, and save you time as you simply go on to another prospect.

As a secondary tactic, just asking can cast doubt. Say, "What do you think of their service?" You're not knocking your rival, but it sounds just a little as if you know it isn't perfect. The reply might help you identify chinks in the relationship that you can use to strengthen your own case.

In practice

- Certainly this is an area in which to take care. Your instinct may be to rubbish the competition (especially if you know you can make a stronger case), but it's wiser to take a more considered approach.

57 AVOID GIVING A DISCOUNT

EVERYONE LIKES A bargain. What is more, customers have been led to expect that prices vary. Take airfares: go to a dozen websites and travel agents, and you will find yourself looking at a dozen different prices. Many of them are likely to be for exactly the same flight, airline, and so on. In this environment shopping around is the norm, and so too is asking for a discount. How do you either stop the question being asked, or resist the suggestion when it comes?

The idea

From among others a menswear shop . . .

This is a problem area, and not one that is addressed by any one magic formula (is anything?). But this idea works well in certain circumstances. Wherever price varies in the way it does in, say, a car showroom—each car gets you from A to B, but different models and specifications cost different amounts—you need to check what the customer is thinking about price. Asking "What's your budget?" is likely to cause people to clam up (they know that declaring their hand makes negotiation more difficult). So as the customer investigates, asks questions, and comes toward a choice, there is another tactic to use. It works too in areas where a number of different products are being selected together. Perhaps the customer is buying an outfit: suit, shirt, tie, shoes, and suchlike.

Once the prospect is considering an option, price it in terms of an estimate. "That specification would cost around £1,200: how does that sound?" You may get good information in return. If the answer is an out-and-out "Way too expensive," you could turn them to look at a less expensive option. If it's "Sounds about right" or the like, you can use it to avoid getting into negotiation over discounts. That's particularly true when you've rounded up the estimate, so the final price is less than has already been agreed as acceptable in principle.

In practice

- Pick your moment for asking this kind of question. The customer needs to be in the process of decision making.

- It is also important to use the right sequence here. Agree the estimate, then use that agreement to avoid debate about a final price. "That's a little less than what you looked at/agreed to earlier" makes a positive point.

58 PROMISES, PROMISES

WE ALL LIKE it when someone makes and keeps a promise. We expect them to keep it, and it is, well, nice when they do. In selling and doing business with customers many promises are made: to deliver on a particular day, allow time for payment, give an extra discount. Some of them are large and significant promises. You have to keep them, and usually you do. If the company fails to deliver on anything like this, for instance not producing the goods on a particular day when the customer needs them, it matters, and you will find yourself with a complaint to handle; and quite right too.

You can also use promises that are not so major to help you sell successfully.

The idea

This thought is prompted by rather fewer good experiences than might be hoped for . . .

A promise kept does not just satisfy the customer on the particular matter to which it relates; it also sends out signals. While the major things tend to be accepted as givens—delivery promised for the 25th and made on the 25th—little things are viewed differently. Yet "smaller" things can have a big impact, and many small things quickly mount up. Promise to ring back by 2:30pm, and you must do just that. Promise to have an email in the customer's in-box within an hour and it must be there. Yet it is precisely such "little" things that can be missed. Something happens, and it's 2:45 when you ring. But somehow you figure you meant "about" 2:30, and you don't even apologize, telling yourself there's no harm done.

Customers regard such things as a sign that goes way beyond the import of the particular matter. First, they want to deal with someone who is reliable. The effect is cumulative: if you keep many small promises, it gives a good, positive impression. It enhances your profile, and makes trust and agreement more likely. And vice versa, of course. Furthermore, failures in such small matters are seen as a sign—an unwelcome sign—of likely future inattention to detail. Let a customer down on one thing, and they are entitled to say, "What else don't they bother about?"

In practice

- Resolve to take this issue seriously, and it will work effectively for you. Go on—promise yourself you will.

59

MAXIMIZE YOUR COLLECTION OF USEFUL INFORMATION

INFORMATION IS POWER, as the saying has it. In selling this is certainly true, and it follows that the finding-out process—identifying customer needs—is a key one. Not least, it helps in dealing with competition. If you find out more and more thoroughly about a customer than a competitor does, then everything you have to do thereafter will be easier (and it'll be more difficult for the competitor if they have failed to discover key facts).

The idea

From residential conference center Highgate House . . .

This establishment is one of the best places in Britain to hold a conference or meeting. I have visited and used it many times wearing my training hat. Successful operators in this field must offer excellent facilities and service, but also, in selling themselves, must recognize that they are not in the business of meeting rooms and tables and chairs. They are in the business of "helping people make their meetings go well." And that means finding out enough about any meeting someone is thinking of holding to sell (and deliver) the venue as the best place for it. I often arrange meetings, and although I am usually asked what kind of meeting it is, if I say "a training meeting," the only further question is, how many people will attend? The venue staff ask nothing about the topic, the people, the importance, or anything else.

To get fuller information you don't just need to ask careful questions; you also need to provide the opportunity for the customer to talk and explain. The idea here is to use silence as part of the process. On one occasion I observed one of the salespeople at Highgate House get a fuller picture of a meeting than I ever thought possible. She used five separate (open) questions, including such phrases as, "Tell me more about the delegates." After each answer she kept quiet for a moment rather than moving straight on to another question— and in each case the pause prompted the customer to fill out their answer a little more. Just a few seconds may do the job, but it needs longer than instinct normally dictates. On this occasion, she was able to use the full picture she had uncovered to get an order. Surely saying nothing to sell more is about as easy as it gets.

In practice

* Questioning is at the heart of overall sales technique, and is worth examining in context. (My book *Outsmarting Your Competitors*, Marshall Cavendish Books, reviews the whole area of sales technique.)

ENHANCE YOUR PROFILE AS A PROFESSIONAL

ALL SALESPEOPLE WANT to be seen as professional. That's sensible enough, but "professional" is an umbrella term, and we must ask what characteristics are perceived as making someone seem professional, and making people believe that they are.

In part, achieving this is a question of enhancing or making visible the various characteristics that will work for you. But maybe it is worth considering something else, something that publicly labels you as professional.

The idea

From the Chartered Institute of Marketing . . .

It's worth taking what you do seriously, both to enhance your profile, and as part of your ongoing development. If selling is what you do, consider whether you should join the professional body in this field. The Chartered Institute of Marketing (CIM) has been around for a long time. It actually started life in the area of selling (before the term marketing had entered the dictionary, in fact) as the Sales Managers Association. It is a worldwide organization, and has more than 50,000 members.

Membership is by election, and linked to qualifications. Members can put letters after their name—for example, on their business card—and membership provides a plethora of other benefits. These range from a magazine to meetings arranged via branches, which provide a regular opportunity for learning and networking. One possible way of becoming a member is via the Institute of

Professional Sales, originally a separate body, but now an integrated part of the CIM, which focuses exclusively on salespeople and the sales process. You can check out the full details at www.cim.co.uk

In practice

- A professional membership can augment your image, and offers an ongoing opportunity to enhance your knowledge and skills.

- Check other professional bodies that are relevant to you too. Many sectors have a variety of professional bodies that can fulfill this purpose.

NOT AT YOUR CONVENIENCE

SOMETIMES SALESPEOPLE FAIL to achieve the results they want, not because they fail to assess what would work best for the client, but more because the best way to sell the product or service is inherently a tad complicated. Whether an idea works needs to be judged first at the customer end of the telescope. If it works for them, then provided whatever it is is cost-effective, then it should usually be made a priority; anything else surely risks diluting effectiveness. Some companies embrace this principle without compromise.

The idea

From Concord Trust Company . . .

This organization is a major player in the world of financial services, and specializes in advising wealthy clients on their finances. It certainly does not subscribe to the idea that the way selling is done must be convenient for the sales staff. It may not be: so be it. What matters is that the approach is organized to maximize the likelihood of reaching agreement, and doing so in a way that customers find acceptable. Concord Trust finds that many wealthy people manage their finances on a rather ad hoc basis. So it organizes meetings that get the financial adviser and the client around the table together with the client's accountant, lawyer, or any other professional adviser who can sensibly be involved. Then all the bits of the jigsaw can be considered and discussed together. A question raised by one person may be answered on the spot by someone else, which avoids delays, and a good argument by one participant can be supported by others as the client listens.

This is certainly much more difficult and time-consuming to arrange than just taking the client out to lunch. But it is worth it, in terms of both what can be done and client perception. Managing director Henry Feldman described it to *Professional Marketing* magazine like this: "when professionals do this they immediately transform themselves from railroad managers to transportation professionals in the eyes of their client." The moral here is clear.

In practice

- Selling must take place in whatever way achieves the objectives.

- Resenting the fact that what works best is inconvenient or difficult is not one of the options.

- Ignoring it allows sales to be lost by default.

- If things can be made simpler, fine—if not, so be it. But do not knowingly dilute sales effectiveness.

ASSESS COMPETITORS' SALES PERFORMANCE

A KEY CHALLENGE in selling is to handle your sales meetings in a way that buyers find they like. They should ideally like it better than the methods of other salespeople with whom they deal (either direct competitors, or people who sell something different to the same buyers). If you knew more about what others do and how they do it, then maybe it would help you decide the best tactics for you, especially if that knowledge included knowing how buyers react to other people's pitches.

The idea

From the world of retail selling . . .

One characteristic of selling to retailers is that in many cases, especially in small and medium-sized businesses, the sales meeting is not held in a comfortable office. It takes place out in the store, perhaps even alongside the till, where the conversation must pause every time a customer approaches with a query or goods they want to buy. This is how the book trade often works. If you bought this book in a bookstore, then think about how it got on the shelf. A rep might have sold it via the head office of a chain like Borders, or they might have run through a list of titles with the buyer of an individual outlet. If so, it was almost certainly done out in the store.

This means anyone in that industry can eavesdrop on the reps of competitors, and assess both what they do and how they do it, together with observing how the buyer seems to react to it. It really is not difficult. Browsing is axiomatic in a bookstore: just loiter within earshot and appear to be checking books in whatever display you are near. These days many stores provide seating for just that purpose, so you can do it in comfort. The same kind of thing is possible in many retail environments.

In practice

- While you should not let this become a time-consuming activity, if you listen in on other reps' pitches from time to time it is highly likely that you will learn something interesting and useful that can affect your own approach. I have even seen someone do this, then admit it to the other salesperson, and offer to buy them a cup of coffee to compare notes. It makes sense.

WHEN THE CUSTOMER DOES NOT LIKE YOU

IT WOULD BE a dull old world if everyone were the same, so it is no great surprise that we do not get on equally well with everyone we meet. This does not matter much, if at all, in some circumstances. If you never see again the guy you sat next to flying to a holiday in Madeira, or even distant cousin Mary, you can no doubt live with it. But customers are different. You need to get on with them, certainly in terms of a businesslike relationship (even if you do not want to invite them to dinner), or you risk losing business. Realistically, though, you are not going to hit it off with everyone, and there may be a few—be honest—where the relationship you want is a nonstarter. What do you do then?

The idea

From a graphic design company . . .

Something I have seen in a number of businesses (so the graphic designers are just an example) demands some honesty among people, but can pay dividends. It can be initiated independently one on one, or it might for example involve a manager at a sales meeting. The idea is, you pass the "difficult" customer on to someone else.

Two things need to be said immediately about this. First, you need to consider the logistics. It is no good trying to arrange for a colleague to see one of your customers if it makes for a complicated and time-consuming journey. Second, you cannot expect to dump your difficult customers on others just like that. The way to do it is to swap. If you have a customer you think would be better dealt with by someone else, get your chosen colleague to exchange them for a customer with whom they have a similar sort of difficulty. In this way you can lose a customer who is perhaps awkward or difficult for you to deal with, and the company may gain extra business because both parties now make a success of the "new" customer.

In practice

- With clear communication with the customer this can work well for everyone, not least the customer.

- Don't feel bad about it. It's just human nature that sometimes you don't get on with people. (Although if none of your customers can get on with you, then maybe you should consider some other line of work!)

WORK THE LOGISTICS

Sometimes it is difficult to meet with customers. The locations are far apart, and compromises must be made about when and where you get together. This is especially the case when relationships are good. I deal with one person on a regular basis, but meet him perhaps two or three times a year. I like to do business face to face, but because I know it is complicated for him to travel to me, there is a danger of my not requesting a meeting when it might help us both. A solution came at the salesperson's initiative.

The idea

With my own "buying hat" on . . .

From my salesperson's standpoint, if he's to retain my business he needs regular contact with me. He knows I live 50 miles northeast of London, and travel to London regularly for meetings and so on. We now have the habit of meeting at London's Liverpool Street station, timing our meetings to fit in with my train times. So if I'm in town for a meeting in the morning, we might meet for an hour at 1pm, allowing me to catch the 2:08pm train back afterward. This suits me well: I have to be at the station anyway. And it suits him pretty well: he too has to be in the city regularly, and this is much more time-efficient than a long journey to sit with me at my desk. The other thing I like is that he does the exploring. He'll ask, "When are you next in town? Could we meet after your meeting? What time will it finish?" He'll even look up the train timetable, and say, "That would let you catch the 2:08. How would that suit?"

A big business lunch is not appropriate for the kind of business we do. We meet where we can have a cup of tea (and sometimes a cake), and it makes for a civilized meeting, which he very much hosts.

In practice

- Whatever you do to fit in with your customers' work pattern and logistics, this kind of approach makes sense, is appreciated, and can work for both parties—and help build both relationships and sales.

DRAMATICALLY MEMORABLE

No DOUBT YOU work at creating a positive persona and profile for yourself with your customers. If you do so, they will think of you as professional. They may know other details about you too: where you live, something of your family, the fact that you have a new car, or recently went on holiday to America. If customers have a general picture of you as a person, it may help enhance your image, but can you do more?

The idea

This was prompted by the television news station Channel NewsAsia . . .

As I write this I am appearing regularly on an overseas morning program on Channel NewsAsia to talk about building a successful career. This is linked to my book *Detox Your Career* (which is also published by Cyan/Marshall Cavendish Books, and sets out an action plan of active career management to help you survive and thrive in the competitive workplace. Buy one soon—sorry, another plug and an example of persistence!). There are posters in bookstores in Singapore and other parts of Southeast Asia featuring my picture, and the description "Channel NewsAsia's Career Guru." Fame at last? Hardly! It is doubtless transient, but such things do have an effect on your personal profile. I write books not only because it earns me money, but also because the profile it gives me makes it easier to sell other things that I do.

Matters much more routine than a brief appearance on television can do this job if you tell people about them. You might run a marathon for charity, write an article for a trade journal, join an industry body committee, speak at a technical conference in your field, or more: all such things can be worthwhile, and assist in building a profile that facilitates your selling successfully.

Such things may be directly related to your product, job, and organization, or be more general. You can seek out opportunities that match well, but even peripheral things can assist. A very different book of mine was published just before this one—a humorous book of travel writing, titled *First Class at Last!* (watch out for it)—and one of the things I have been thinking about as I plan promotional activities for its publication is how I can link it to other aspects of my work. Such links all help. Enough plugs; point made.

In practice

- The starting point is to think, honestly, about how you are seen now.

- Then consider activities that would boost your image in whatever area needs strengthening. Even if something like television is an impossible dream, you can find smaller things that can have the desired effect.

UNDERSTAND CUSTOMERS' CULTURE

THE WORLD IS large and varied, and so are the customers in it. At home or abroad, salespeople should study how culture affects personal relationships.

The idea

As an example consider a single country, albeit one that may appear somewhat alien to Englishmen like me . . .

Japanese businesspeople tend to be well traveled, are group-oriented, and are rather formal in their dealings with each other. To start well when selling to Japanese people, you need to remember a number of things. Do not overdo eye contact, shake hands only if a hand is offered to you (and do not try to bow in Japanese style, although a sincere nod of the head is appreciated), use titles with names, and make sure that careful use of language ensures understanding, checking as necessary. Business cards are much used (yours should have a Japanese translation on the reverse).

The Japanese have a tendency to check details. You quote a delivery date, and they will want to speak to those involved in implementing it, to reassure themselves that it is seen as possible. The Japanese always try to conceal their emotions, hate losing face, and are uncomfortable if others (you) lose control, for instance showing anger or impatience. You must show respect and patience, and any business transaction is, in part, seen as a pursuit of harmony.

You need to always use language carefully, and you should not act immediately to fill silences, as taking a moment over things is normal. Politeness and consideration are valued, and personal touches (things like a thank-you note, or small gifts—you should ask before unwrapping if they are given to you) are seen as very much a part of building relationships.

Specifically they expect considerable detail about any matter being discussed, and will look on an overview, or seemingly vague or disorganized information, with suspicion: it might be read as evasion. They appreciate, indeed expect, good support material (what you see as sales aids)—anything from plans and graphs to summaries of details dealt with. Japanese customers will most likely expect you to deal with a group of people, so you must relate to the whole group, even those taking less part or less able to speak English (if that is the language being used). The differences from a Western approach are considerable, and even a snapshot like this is sufficient to show that some research is necessary, and likely to pay dividends.

Such detail, and more, is necessary whenever you focus on a market that involves a different culture. (The *CultureShock!* series of books make good references.)

In practice

- Whatever group your customers belong to may be worth investigating.

- Culture and nationality are obvious differentiators, but there may be other groupings where acquiring knowledge about them helps the sales process.

ADMIN RULES OK

Selling to people is a personal business, often one on one; it is dependent to some extent on personalities and relationships. It is influenced by how the salesperson approaches matters, the techniques they use, and such things as the perceived degree of pushiness. But alongside all that there is a thread of more physical and mundane matters: appointment times are set, literature is sent, arrangements are confirmed, and all this creates—or should do—an aura of efficiency. This is not simply important in itself: the level of prevailing efficiency is taken by the customer as a predictor of service to come. So shortfalls in your admin can act to dilute the effectiveness of what you do in selling.

The idea

From the pharmaceutical industry . . .

Consider a cautionary tale. A pharmaceutical company was holding a sales meeting for doctors. It had chosen a suitable venue, and everything was well arranged: documentation, catering, and so on. The company executives were well practiced in their presentations. The PowerPoint slides contained only a manageable amount of text, and not a single one was projected upside down.

At one point the doctors were introduced to a topic that was to be dealt with by showing a 20-minute video movie. An executive introduced it, the lights were dimmed, and the movie was started. Most of the staff present slipped out of the room (they had seen the movie a dozen times), and only one person was left with the group. When the movie ended, the room was plunged into total darkness (there were no windows), and the only remaining staff member had no idea where the lights were, since someone else, not now in the room, had dimmed them at the start. He groped fruitlessly around the walls for more than five minutes. Finally a colleague returned, located the light switch in the light from the open door, and the meeting resumed. It went well, but this was enough for participants to refer to the "meeting in the dark" for many months.

It is so simple to miss something. I rather feel for whoever wrote the computer manual beside my desk, which has a boxed paragraph on the title page reading:

This manual has been for any errors.

In practice

- Remember all the administrative details linked to selling matter. Any one of them, if neglected, can reduce the effectiveness of matters that have been given more thought and are considered more important.

- The lesson is simple: check, check, and check again.

68   GET OUT OF HERE

A BREAK CAN do you good. The right sort of break can do your sales results some good.

The idea

From the world of training . . .

Here is something that will perhaps be regarded as something of a luxury. But it can have real value, and be cost-effective too. It can take various forms, but in one company I worked with (now taken over and merged away), one category of senior people were allowed to take six months' (paid) leave after working with the company for a certain number of years. In consultancy—a fee-earning and time-dependent business—this represented a significant cost. However, it was a business in which many people did not habitually take long holidays, so in some ways the time off was a quid pro quo.

Certainly it was highly motivational, both to those entitled to the break and to those who aspired to be. I cannot now remember whether it was compulsory, but the extended periods of leave often included a project, something to which no time would otherwise have been given. For example, people sometimes wanted to travel, and this linked usefully to the international development of the business. They were able to carry out more leisurely research and investigation than might otherwise have been done. If this was coupled with some fee-earning work, it made good sense all round. I had my six months, and in the course of it I attended a major training conference and exhibition in America. It proved a wonderful learning experience.

In practice

Among the aspects that could be varied are the:

- Duration selected (it could be quite short).

- Number and level of staff involved.

- Purpose (or lack of it) given to the gap period—in this context it might be focused on sales, market investigation, or something similar.

- Arrangements for reporting back, if appropriate.

Whether the break is long or short, it's easy to think of all sorts of things this system could be used for, and one is certainly development. This is something else to seek out or suggest, perhaps, with an eye on longer-term skills and sales development.

69

WITH A LITTLE HELP FROM A FRIEND

Who else can help you improve your selling?

The idea

From a training company . . .

A mentor is someone who exercises a low-key and informal developmental role. More than one person can be involved in the mentoring of a single individual, and while what they do is akin to some of the things a manager should do, more typically a mentor is specifically not the person's manager. It might be someone more senior, someone on the same level, or someone from elsewhere in the organization. An effective mentor can be a powerful force in your development. So how do you get yourself a mentor?

In some organizations this is a regular part of ongoing development. You may be allocated one, or able to request one. In other organizations you may need to initiate a mentoring relationship. You can suggest it to your manager, or direct to someone you think might undertake the role.

What makes a good mentor? The person must have authority (this might mean they are senior, or just that they are capable and confident), suitable knowledge and experience, counseling skills, appropriate clout, and a willingness to spend some time with you (if they have mentored others, it may be a positive sign). Finding that time can be a challenge, but it is generally worthwhile.

You and your mentor typically have a series of informal meetings, which together create a thread of activity alongside your work. These meetings need an agenda (albeit an informal one), but more importantly they need to be constructive. If they are, then one thing will naturally lead to another, and various occasions can be utilized to maintain the dialogue. A meeting, followed by a brief encounter as people pass on the stairs, a project and a promise to spend a moment on feedback, an email or two passing in different directions—all may contribute.

I have been lucky enough to have someone mentoring me for many years, so I know that sometimes just a few minutes spent together can crack a problem or lead to a new initiative. Such an arrangement could well enhance your ability to sell effectively.

In practice

- What makes this process useful is the commitment and quality of the mentor. Where such relationships can be set up, and where they work well, they may not cover every developmental issue, but they can add a powerful dimension to the ongoing cycle of development, one that it is difficult to imagine being bettered in any other way.

- As both parties become familiar with the arrangement, and with each other, it can become highly productive.

70

EN ROUTE TO SUCCESS

PRODUCTIVITY IS IMPORTANT, and the nature of a field sales job dictates that there is inevitably some idle time. There's time spent traveling to the customer (and trying to find somewhere to park), time ahead of a meeting waiting for people in their reception areas, and so on. At worst salespeople can work hard and still find that only 20–25 percent of their working time is actually spent face to face with customers; it goes with the territory. Enough said, or is there?

The idea

For those with a company car . . .

Given the problem of productivity, you should at least consider the way you work and see what possibilities this suggests for productivity improvement. One example that applies to anyone driving to customers makes a good point. How far do you drive each year? Or perhaps more relevantly, given today's traffic conditions, how long do you spend in the car? Listening to the radio or to music may dull the tedium of a long journey, but it will not help you sell more. You could spend some of the time doing something more useful (and much safer than talking on a mobile phone, which must be hands-free if you use it in the car at all).

Virtually all cars have a tape or CD player in them, and a wealth of useful material is available in this form. Specifically:

- Some companies issue newsletters or product briefings or training in this form. (If not, maybe you should suggest it.)

- A variety of business books and magazines are available too.

- Sales training material is also available, including audio seminar "tutorials," case studies, and inspirational material.

In practice

- Time spent listening to such material can be useful, interesting, and stress-busting (making you forget that traffic jam about which you can do nothing). It can provide a constructive moment, and even one useful thought sparked on a journey may pay dividends.

- Keep a notepad handy too (but wait until you stop to record ideas). If you run out of this kind of material, maybe you should consider a long-term project. For example, you could learn a language. Just press the "play" button and away you go.

71 DON'T BE TOTALLY SELF-SUFFICIENT

THIS AND THE next two ideas link to how you and your boss work together (whoever your boss is: in a large company it is likely a sales manager or director). By its nature the field sales job is one in which people must be self-sufficient, and where a great deal of time is spent alone and away from base. Tacitly or otherwise, your organization's culture might suggest that you should be self-sufficient. Indeed your boss may have said the equivalent of, "Don't bother me all the time, get out there and sell."

The idea

From many a well-managed sales operation . . .

On the other hand two heads are often better than one. Consider ongoing counseling, which usually involves accompanied calling, evaluation, and a link to development of all sorts. Most managers will evaluate what any salesperson is doing and what results they are getting. While a bad manager may see this as just looking at the figures and shouting when targets are missed, many see this role more constructively. They take the view that even the best performance can be improved, and act to do just that.

The most practical way in which this happens is through joint calling. The manager will link attending some calls with you, ideally on a regular basis, with a counseling session to review strengths and weaknesses. (This is sometimes called "the curbside conference" as it sometimes takes place in the car after a call.) This can seem intrusive, but remember it is the only way in which they can observe and investigate how you do things. (Sitting at their desk they can only see the figures: what comes from what you do.) So this is something to be approached constructively. Take on board what they say, but—and this is the crux of the idea—ask questions, try things out on them, and use them as a sounding board.

In practice

- Selling can be a lonely business—make use of time spent to analyze and help take your approaches and skills forward.

- This is a sales-specific form of what is more generally called "training on the job." Similarly, do not hesitate to ask for advice or an opinion, maybe with just a telephone call, if this might make the difference between getting an order and not getting it.

- Do be careful, however, not to ask the same thing twice.

72 THE UBIQUITOUS SALES MEETING

IF I ASK many salespeople about sales meetings held in their organizations, they raise an eyebrow, sigh deeply, and say, "Oh dear." And they may not be so polite. Nevertheless sales meetings should help you sell better. If they don't, it may be the sign of a poor manager, but even so maybe you can make suggestions, or take an initiative.

The idea

Again from many well-run sales teams . . .

Every so often, the sales team gets together. This might happen weekly, monthly—whatever, with the frequency dependent on such factors as cost and geography. However often this happens, you want to get the most from it. Again a good manager will see this as an opportunity to inform, motivate, gather, and exchange ideas—and undertake development activities. It is sometimes a problem to keep such meetings fresh. They can settle into a repetitive format and a bit of a rut. So do not be backward in making suggestions, or volunteering to initiate action in this area. (You might collaborate with colleagues, so you can say to your manager, "A number of us think . . .") A number of things are possible:

- Training games and exercises: these are designed to focus attention on one particular aspect of the job. This might include something as simple as a quiz to check product knowledge, through to elaborate, often team, exercises, or viewing a training movie.

- Role playing: this is a classic way of experimenting with an interactive skill like selling. Simple versions of it can be used in just a few minutes in a sales meeting.

- Brainstorming: as a route to generating ideas this can work well (although it needs to be properly set up and carried out).

If cases and particular customer situations are discussed, then there is merit in volunteering examples. If you think about what you might use beforehand and introduce something with a clear, succinct statement, you'll come across well, and also gather valuable ideas that link back to the specifics of your territory. Things such as brainstorming may need some separate investigation to see exactly how they work, but with some groundwork, much is possible, and "death by sales meeting" may be averted.

In practice

- This is a big topic. In practice many of those conducting sales team meetings are busy, and too often meetings happen without adequate thought, just on automatic pilot.

- They are potentially of major value, and can influence sales positively to a high degree.

- So a final word to all sales managers with this responsibility— prepare to make them have a positive effect.

73 MOTIVATION AS A CATALYST

IT IS AGAIN the nature of the sales job that it can be repetitive. One call follows another, and many may involve saying essentially the same thing to each customer. I have already recommended tailoring the sales message, but the point remains. Because of this repetition and because there is often a low level of contact with head office, motivation is particularly important for salespersonnel. And quite right too, you may say. It is possible that you would do better if you were better motivated (although you might be highly motivated already, of course). So can you stimulate the motivation process?

The idea

From electronics retail giant Richer Sounds . . .

Recently a colleague of mine bought a new television from this retail chain. He was impressed with the service and the selling—it was a purchase that needed to come with some sound advice—and was telling people at a committee meeting we both attend about it in very positive terms. Credit where credit is due: and there is nothing like word-of-mouth recommendation. He had been so impressed, in fact, that he had quizzed one of the sales staff about just why the service was so good. The overall message was that Richer Sounds was a great company to work for.

It was also clear that motivation schemes were well in evidence, and the salesperson described to him one scheme that involved the company Bentley. As an award for sales excellence, one of the team had the use of a quality car for a period. The scheme was clearly well matched to the people it was designed for (and did not result in inappropriate pushy selling that might put customers off). Everyone gained, not least the customer.

This might provide a good example to mention to your manager. If a company like Richer Sounds can go to these lengths, there is surely room for things to be taken further in your organization.

In practice

- This is another area that can only be progressed via sales management.

- A good sales manager can make average salespeople excellent, but it does not just happen. In this case, finding the right incentive (just part of the process) needs careful consideration.

PUT VALUE ON INFORMATION ABOUT THE CUSTOMER

THE IMPORTANCE OF asking questions and listening to the answers has already been stressed. So too has the need to tailor, and be seen to be tailoring, the case you make to an individual customer. One simple mechanism helps you do this, and makes a positive impression on the customer too.

The idea

Catching the details . . .

To be fair many salespeople do this, but if they do not, it can send all the wrong signals. Remember first that people's sense of individuality is strong. We all think of ourselves as being unlike other people. And we want others to understand and take these differences into account. Certainly this is true of buyers and sellers.

For example, I wear spectacles, and have just had an eye test. Very thorough it was, too. I would not have been much impressed if I had walked in, perhaps been asked to read a couple of lines of text, and then been told, "Right, I know exactly the prescription you need." I want a thorough check. And believing it is a complex and individual matter, I was pleased to see the optician completing a detailed form as the test progressed. So too with selling. Whenever any degree of complexity is involved, always take notes during your conversation; and remember to base your judgment about complexity on your customer's apparent perception of the situation, not on your own.

It may be polite to ask permission to do this, especially if confidential information is involved, as is often the case in my business. You should always make it clear what is happening. Customers like it, you may need a moment to let your note-taking catch up with the conversation, and where appropriate, it should be a noticeable part of the whole process. Take time too to check what you have written promptly, perhaps highlighting key details in a second color. It is easy to find that after a few days, and after holding several (many?) more customer meetings, you are unsure exactly what some of your notes mean.

In practice

- Now make a note of this: get yourself a notebook or pad and make recording key details part of your routine with customers. One fact remembered rather than overlooked can sometimes lead to the sealing of an agreement that might otherwise be stillborn.

75 | TAKE A LONG-TERM VIEW

IT IS AN old maxim of the world of selling that the job is not to make a sale, but to make a customer. The implication is that the business you obtain over the longer term is more important than clinching a single deal today, and there is certainly some good sense in this view. Sometimes this philosophy can be taken to extremes, and still make sense.

Let me prefix this idea by summarizing my experience with the cellphone company Vodafone. I have just wasted at least two hours of my time discovering that it cannot supply what I want. I went into a local store to ask, and was told the company could do what I wanted, but only via a bigger store. I emailed the company and (eventually) got a reply saying this was the case. In London a little later, another store told me it could only sort out my problem by telephone. When I was home again, I telephoned. Nobody needs all the details: after endless holding, several transfers, and my demanding to speak to a manager, I was told the company did not do what I wanted at all. You can guess what this experience did for the likelihood of my doing business with Vodafone in the future, especially as at the end of the call I declared my intention to write about my experience, and gave the operative my telephone number so there was a chance for someone else to ring me and try to put things right. I heard nothing.

The idea

From cellphone company Orange . . .

After this incident I telephoned Orange. It took one call, one person, and a few minutes. I got a clear explanation, some suggestions, and—and here is the idea—firm advice that I should not buy anything at present. "The cost is disproportionate for what you want," I was told. "You would not feel it was good value." Not only was I not sold anything, I was specifically recommended not to buy anything! Technology should give me new options in the future— and guess where I will be asking about them.

In practice

- The Orange salesperson sacrificed a sale now for a larger sale in future—and some good references in the meantime (including the one in this book!). The moral is clear: customers are more likely to rate, and buy from, people who display this attitude.

76 BRAG, BUT DO SO CONVINCINGLY

CUSTOMERS WANT TO know that you are competent, knowledgeable, and generally "know your stuff." Only then do they feel able to deal with you with confidence. You need to tell them, but out-and-out bragging can not only sound unsuitable—"He's just a braggart"—but also risks your not being believed. For example, if I was selling you my training services, and said to you, "I've been involved in sales training for more than 20 years, there's really nothing about it that I don't know, and that's a promise," you would be entitled, indeed sensible, to take it with a pinch of salt, and wonder about my communications skills.

The idea

From the world of professional services . . .

If, on the other hand, I gave you reasons why I considered myself an expert, it might well be more credible. Perhaps I would say to you, "When I first joined a training company I spent a long time sitting in on courses and talking to those leading them about why they were conducted in the way they were, before my then boss would let me anywhere near fronting an event. It was drummed into me that I would spend the rest of my time in training continuing to learn about the process. More than 20 years on, I know that's true—but I've now had a great deal of experience."

Something along these lines is much more an explanation than a boast. It contains reasons for you to believe me, and makes it seem that my current state of expertise is both hard won (it was!) and useful. This is often done well by people in professional services (accountants, lawyers, architects, and more). These are areas of business that came late to marketing, but are now operating in very competitive markets.

In practice

- This principle is useful for anyone, especially if you need to project an element of experience and (perhaps technical) expertise.

- It needs some conscious thought to avoid the reflex of just blurting out how good you think you are.

USE COMPLAINTS AS A SPRINGBOARD

EVEN THE BEST-RUN companies get some complaints. It may be to do with the product, the service that goes with it, or such matters as delivery or technical support. The first way in which to see complaints is as a source of information. They constitute feedback that must be noted: lessons must be learned, and action taken to stop the situation from recurring. Sometimes a complaint is a one-off, and only affects one customer (although it may be nonetheless annoying or costly for them because of that). Sometimes too, complaints make the news: in one instance, batteries supplied for laptop computers were allegedly causing the machines to catch fire. The cost was likely to have been tens, perhaps hundreds, of millions of pounds.

While we would all rather no complaints occurred, when they do they must be handled constructively, and the best made of the situation.

The idea

From motor manufacturer Mercedes Benz . . .

I pick an example here that is safely in the past of the company involved. Satisfactorily behind them is perhaps a better way of putting it. After the Mercedes small model A car first appeared, its early models were recalled. This was not because it had an annoying squeak or a wonky door. It was because when it was driven around a corner—it fell over! (OK, I probably exaggerate, but I want an example of a serious fault.) Yet now this company's reputation for excellence seems wholly unblemished. In the immediate aftermath a good many complaints must have been fielded effectively. This is not the place to review complaint-handling techniques in detail: what I want to stress is that the response should be done openly, address the problem head on, and sort it out. With the car example, the company did not make excuses or blame others; it said, in effect, we got it wrong, we're sorry, and here's how we will sort it out.

In practice

- Too often the instinct, particularly among salespeople fielding complaints that are no fault of their own, is to instantly avoid blame: a response that often begins, "Ah, but . . ." Avoid this.

- Be open, apologize, and do so personally: "I am so sorry," not, "It's those idiots in dispatch again." Provided the problem is sorted out, you can move on to sell again, and do so successfully.

78

AGREE THE IMPOSSIBLE

PRICE IS ALWAYS a sensitive issue in selling. Buyers want value for money, they want a bargain, and they may want to negotiate. They might unashamedly challenge the price you quote in order to try to obtain a better one. Indeed they may well genuinely reckon the original price is too high, and be unprepared to buy at that level. So faced with a challenge on price, what do you do?

The idea

From direct computer provider Dell . . .

When customers say the price is too high, they may well intend it to close the conversation: it is too high for them, and they will not buy, and that's it. If you agree with them—"You are right, Mr Customer, the price is way too high"—that will probably be the last thing they expect. Although they had closed their minds to further debate, they now open them again and want to know what's going on.

Of course, there's more to this idea than just agreeing. Although you might say this, it will not be what you mean, and you must continue the conversation in a way that makes this clear. This is a technique that works well with any product going through technological change, something that is permanently the case with computers. This may not be a technique you meet in every branch of a retail chain, but I have heard it used well by Dell. How does it work? The salesperson might explain, yes, it is a high price for a computer, but not for a laptop that can be used on the move, or (going into more detail) for a laptop with such an exceptionally long battery life as this one.

In other words the price is described as high if the product were much less valuable than it is, but as necessary, understandable, good even, for what the product actually is. Then your description locks it in to key benefits.

In practice

- Any important feature may be highlighted to make this approach fit, and it can work well for a range of products and services.

- Not only does it work, it also surprises, and customers concentrate at once when you agree with something that they had expected would start an argument. It's an idea that can move a sales conversation from stalemate to discussion and agreement.

79

FOCUS ON USERS

FOR MOST SUCCESSFUL products there are lots of good things to say about them. They have all the latest technology and design, and are well proven in use. You may well say that not only is this the case with your products, you are well practiced in differentiating features and benefits, and talking about them in the right kind of way. Sometimes, however, it is possible to sell successfully without mentioning any of that. So what do you do instead?

The idea

From a computer service agency . . .

People who will never use them personally buy many products, from the office photocopier to a huge piece of construction machinery. The staff at work around the office use the copier, and the road builders or whatever are driven by professional drivers. And it is these people who provide an avenue for this approach to selling. Take the example of a specialist service, a computer troubleshooting outfit (I use an excellent one, which once rescued me when I thought I had lost the text of an entire, but undelivered, book).

The seller might describe the service in detail: the frequency of checks, the time taken to send a technician to arrive in an emergency, what is covered in a contractual arrangement and what is not, and much more. But what might best be talked about is not the service itself at all: it is the people working on computers around the organization, and how this service will help them. For instance:

Will it keep them productive?
Will it keep them well motivated?
Will it assist staff retention?

It is, after all, the end result that is most interesting, and most likely to prompt a sale.

In practice

- This kind of focus will differentiate your product or service. In the case above, the salesperson talks about why the service is valuable (classic benefits), but does so very specifically by focusing on the people.

- You can highlight particular points that relate to a particular client. For example, if you know that staff retention is an issue in an organization, then it might be your priority to mention how you can help improve it. This makes the particular service seem better matched to the client than competitive ones where the salesperson just talks about the service.

- Take people out of an organization and there is not much of significance left, so directing an argument in a way that involves them always makes sense.

80 | LOG OBJECTIONS

Objections are ubiquitous in selling. We know we will get some, and we know too, from experience, that they should be regarded as a sign of interest. (No one is going to be bothered to query something they have dismissed out of hand.) We also know that they will vary in topic, nature, and emphasis. Sometimes the same thing crops up repeatedly as a major stumbling block, and on another occasion something might be mentioned in passing, and is not in any sense a major hindrance. What matters is the balance of positive and negative points a customer sees as a case is presented. It is not realistic to try to have nothing on the negative side: when did you last buy something perfect? But the positive side must weigh most heavily in the balance, and what creates that situation may be a number of major points (heavy ones, to stick with the weighing-up analogy), and a number of smaller ones too. Indeed, because it is impossible sometimes to balance one major point with another, several smaller ones may have to do the job.

Whatever else you do, you should be ready for objections.

The idea

Quizzing numbers of salespeople who are good at handling objections shows that this skill does not just happen . . .

Occasionally, not often, an objection may surprise you; and if it does, you have to try to be quick on your feet and deal with it. But the majority of objections you receive will be repetitive. The same things recur, and some of them (like price) are common to most selling situations. So make sure that you are ready for them. It is good practice to collect objections—for a week or three, keep a note of every reason people give you for not buying. Then sort them out. Some may need little attention: they will be simple, invalid, or simply so individual that they will rarely or never occur again. The others will fall into various categories. Some will pose the same question, or address the same area, but come at it in a different way. No matter—catalogue the main ones, and check that you are sure how you will deal with them in future. Do you know how to respond? Do you have rebalancing arguments? Can you, where necessary, point out—in an acceptable fashion—that the customer is wrong?

In practice

- Objections should not surprise you. You should be ready for the vast majority of them. This involves undertaking some preparation.

81 MAKE AN EXHIBITION OF YOURSELF

In some circumstances, like at an exhibition, salespeople need to be prepared to take a positive and appropriate initiative. Nobody should ever say "Can I help you?" (to which most say, instinctively, "No thank you"). Nor should you launch into a long and technical explanation replete with jargon. Better start with an open question—in other words, something that does not lend itself to being answered by "Yes" or "No."

The idea

From the aware exhibitor . . .

So say something designed to get people talking:

- What are you hoping to find at the show?

- How much do you know about us?

- Where are you from?

Equally, do not frighten people off. There are probably people jumping out at them every few yards, so remember the purpose of this first initiative is to:

- Make the visitor feel at ease.

- Get them talking.

- Discover their exact interest.

- Identify their needs.

- Get them deciding it is worth spending some time with you.

Try to start with unchallenging openings:

- Introduce yourself by name (this can often result in visitors giving you their name in return).

- Offer a quick demonstration or video explanation of the point attracting attention.

- Discuss their particular point of interest or need.

- Ask general questions to open the conversation, e.g. "What do you use [the product] for?" or "When might you be considering upgrading?"—continuing to favor open questions as you do so.

The overall aim is to move effortlessly into a relaxed and interesting conversation, one that can link to key stages of the sales process, such as identifying needs and focusing on the individual. It is not to hassle people.

In practice

- Focus on getting key prospects into meaningful conversation.

- Remember that not everyone will be worth time and attention. If you establish that someone is not a real prospect, you should still handle them politely (remember, they may become a future customer, or recommend you). If they require information or assistance, give it to them quickly, but do not waste time if the stand is busy. If the stand is quiet, a "just looking" visitor can be valuable—a stand with people already on it tends to encourage others to stop.

A STRONG BRAND

IN AREAS WHERE the brand and brand image is a powerful factor, it is important to actually use that in selling. A strong and positive brand image is an expensive thing to create and maintain, and many well-known brand names have been many years in the making. The obvious way a brand is exploited is through advertising and other promotional activity, but if the brand is well used in selling, it can strengthen sales success.

The idea

From the pen manufacturer Parker Pens . . .

Pens are big business. A large proportion of more expensive pens are bought as presents, and another large part of the market is pens bought as business gifts (they are probably the commonest product used in this way). So while all (well, most) pens write effectively, many sales have more to do with other factors. In this context two factors are whether a pen will make a suitable, and perhaps lasting, gift, showing a degree of care, or help to promote positively a company that uses pens bearing its name as a part of the communications mix.

Less well-known brands are at a disadvantage in this context. Someone may not appreciate being given an unknown brand as a present, and a business person sent a pen as a promotional gift, perhaps at Christmas, will not respond in the right way if they only say, "Another tacky old ballpoint." So the brand is an important part of the sell.

Parker stresses its "pedigree," its quality and reliability, and its image. It can sell you a pen costing hundreds of pounds that will be a memento for life, or a more reasonably priced pen that still has real presence, status, and that will be seen as something worthwhile. In both cases the pen needs to be seen as something to be treasured. It is not the ink or its ability to write that does that, although design is an important part of the appeal: it is the brand image.

In practice

- Branding has been described as providing customers with insurance; this is a good way of looking at it. The brand gives people a measure, something to indicate what their expectations should be, and an assurance that promises made will be met.

- Branding is an asset to anyone selling, and should be used accordingly.

83 USE THAT SALES MEETING

As a consultant I find that asking staff about sales meetings gives me a good idea of the likely quality of a company's sales team. If the response is dismissive ("What a waste of time! Why don't they just let us get on and sell?"), the company probably holds ineffective meetings, and misses the advantages that come from good ones.

The idea

From Prudential Assurance (in Singapore) . . .

Sales meetings should be catalysts to maximize effectiveness. They may review progress and performance, and they should have a positive impact on motivation and team feeling. Dave Tiang, senior unit manager with Prudential Assurance, is quoted as saying, "Team building and bonding can be achieved only when the majority of [the] sales force are running in the same direction. We also take this as a learning experience when we discuss some unique cases."

In other words sales meetings should be constructive occasions. They provide a chance for members of the team to compare notes, for training in sales techniques and product knowledge, and for links to be made with motivational initiatives. While admin is important, as is checking progress against targets, a key area should be to stimulate ideas. How can the team open more accounts, get over an objection that keeps cropping up, respond to initiatives by competition, or secure more prompt payment? These and many other questions can be debated. Several heads can often be better than one—new ideas may surface, and good experience can be passed around.

Of course the responsibility here is with sales management, but the contribution of individual salespeople is vital. The moral for the individual is to take sales meetings seriously, read the agenda and do any necessary preparation, and participate in a way that stimulates others. Everyone can gain from a creative airing of views, and it can be amazing how something that one person mentions as puzzling prompts a ready answer from someone else who has cracked the problem.

In practice

- If you have a sales meeting to attend, make suggestions. Ask for an agenda in advance if one is not offered (perhaps demand one), ask questions, lay problems and solutions on the table, and see how such gatherings can be made to work and to contribute to achieving sales effectiveness and the results that are targeted.

84 NOT JUST LOGICAL

PEOPLE NEED A reason to buy. Especially with technical or complex products, and certainly in areas of industrial and business-to-business purchasing, buyers make logical decisions. They weigh up the evidence and see how something stacks up. They compare one supplier with another. But it is not just logical factors that influence their final decision. What else is involved?

The idea

From world-famous Harvard Business School . . .

Some years ago Harvard Business School carried out research with top American buyers to ascertain how much logic and how much emotion was involved in buying decisions. To many people's surprise the results showed that 84 percent of all buying decisions are based on emotion. Certainly if someone is purchasing something like a wedding gift, or a wedding dress for that matter, one would expect there to be some emotion involved—perhaps a lot. But what about say a heat exchanger, or a forklift truck, or a machine lathe: surely not?

But it is a fact: emotion does matter, and it matters particularly when the package of more technical matters in evidence is evenly balanced between competitors. If there is apparently not much to choose between two (or more) technical cases, people will search for something else that they can use to swing the balance; and the deciding factor can then become emotional. They choose the product because the salesperson selling it remembers their birthday, gets on best with them, makes a point of recognizing that they are pressed for time, or any of a hundred and one little things that make an impression and appeal.

In practice

- Never underrate what may seem to be peripheral factors; indeed you can do worse than to seek some out, especially when you judge that a decision is a finely balanced one.

- For example, if there are a dozen books on the shelf under the heading "Sales," the cover of the one you choose may suddenly become disproportionately important to your choice. That's why I worry about the blurb for something like this volume. It's a common principle.

LET COMPETITION HELP

Most (all?) markets are competitive these days, and it is normal in many businesses for every purchase to be made by buyers in some way weighing up an offering against the competition. There is no way of selling that negates this entirely, although a powerful case may succeed in putting the competition to the back of someone's mind for a while. So your competition will both linger in the background and come up regularly in conversation. Comments or queries about rival products or services must be handled in the right way, and the idea of not knocking the competition is touched on elsewhere in this volume. Other techniques too can be useful.

The idea

From a company selling stationery products . . .

I have come across this in many contexts, but I remember especially one company from which I bought ring binders, which for some time I used on a regular basis for course materials. This is almost a commodity product, as indeed are many other things: that is, many firms make similar things, and perceiving significant differences between them can be difficult. Price and factors such as service and delivery (including emergency supplies) are highly relevant. The idea here is that if your prospect mentions the competition, you should answer very specifically. So in the case of ring binders, a salesperson might say, "You're right, we've certainly got plenty of competition. Other firms of all sorts supply binders: stationery companies, plastics firms, and more. I've counted 22 companies I hear mentioned regularly, and it's never a surprise to hear of a new one." Then you could add something about some of the rivals, or about your own company, majoring for instance on service or delivery reliability. (Of course, you will pick points that are most likely to appeal to that particular customer.)

The point about this sort of answer, one that even specifies how many competitors you know of, is its extent and precision. The idea is that in such a complex market, a buyer will find the idea of checking out the offerings in detail daunting. Maybe—if all is going well with your firm—they will not bother to do it, or will do very little cross-checking. The reply is designed to sound open and confident, which can make a good impression, but also to make it seem that further checking would be difficult, and given the arguments you've made, in any case is unnecessary.

In practice

- A realistic and considered view of what you say about competitors is vital.

- If your reflex response is to put down your rivals, the danger is that it will be taken as showing weakness. This makes selling successfully more difficult.

LONG-TERM CONTACT

SOMETIMES IT IS the case that business does not materialize quickly. We would always like an order now, but the customer will be guided by their timing needs, and it may not be possible to avoid delay. Equally, even a customer who orders and is happy may not reorder immediately. In such circumstances the problem of keeping in touch can be awkward. You have to judge a reasonable frequency, deciding how long you can leave it, and at what point repeated reminders become annoying and thus self-defeating. There is no firm rule here, but one thing is for sure: if you give up on a prospect, the chances of getting business, or more business, diminish dramatically.

As an example from my own work, I set up my business in 1990, and in all the time since, the largest piece of business I have ever booked came from someone I had worked with before, but after a three-year gap. During that time I had made contact nine or ten times, and met with my contact only once. Keeping in touch did not take much time—mostly it was letters, emails, and telephone calls—but it was eminently worthwhile.

The problem here is often more psychological than real. We get bored, dispirited, or cannot quite think what to do next when the business does not come from a contact, and so we move on to something else. Delay too long and the moment passes, and it becomes almost impossible to renew contact.

The idea

From an American Society for Training and Development (ASTD) conference . . .

At a session I attended as part of a conference about training, I heard a speaker describe a scheme in one company that addressed this situation. The details of the diary and follow-up system do not matter. What I liked was the thinking that highlighted the danger, and kept people's minds focused on the need to make considered decisions to keep in touch, and judge the best way to do so, making approaches creative and well timed.

The system (and all its various components) was called the LYBUNT system. LYBUNT stood for Last Year But Unfortunately Not This, a name designed to stop customers getting into this category. It has always stuck in my mind, and prompted a degree more consideration of my persistence.

In practice

- Look after your existing and past customers. Never lose touch with them (except as a considered decision in some cases), or you could allow business to go by default as a result.

87

ON YOUR FEET

NOT ALL SELLING takes place in a one-on-one meeting. It can take place in many situations: in a farmyard (always keep Wellington boots in your car if you're likely to end up in this environment), in a noisy factory, or across the dinner table. Another circumstance is a formal on-your-feet presentation. Then the audience and the scale of the situation can mean there are different things to think—or perhaps worry—about.

A formal presentation is something that needs some thought and planning (remember: the people who make it look easy usually do their homework). There are principles and tricks of the trade, and it's beyond my brief to describe them here (for that, see my book *How to Craft Successful Business Presentations and Effective Public Speaking*, published by Foulsham), but one thing is certain—confidence is a major factor.

The idea

At a conference of a professional management organization . . .

In the formal setting of a presentation, people respond to the speaker's manner. If you look and sound confident, people assume that you are; they assume you know your stuff and are credible. If you create this feeling early on, they may well decide to pay attention. Many things contribute to the impact you make, of course, but sheer confidence—and it's possible to project more than you feel—can certainly contribute real power.

I remember a speaker at a public conference I attended. He was sitting on a platform alongside other speakers and the chair, who introduced him. He rose and began to speak, saying something like, "Ladies and gentlemen, I am going to be talking to you about . . . And in the hour or so I have available, I . . ." At this point the chair tugged his sleeve. The speaker bent down and they whispered together for a moment. Then the speaker, who was holding notes in the form of A4 sheets, stood up and continued, "I'm so sorry, ladies and gentlemen. In the 30 minutes I have available . . ." As he spoke he tore his notes in half lengthways, and tossed half the paper into the air, from where it fluttered to the floor. Some 200 faces around me all said, "Now this may just be good." It may have been contrived, but he had grabbed the audience's attention, and done so in a way that had nothing whatsoever to do with his topic.

In practice

- The same thing is true of any on-your-feet occasion: get their attention, then sell.

- Do not underrate what needs to be done, either in equipping yourself to be able to make good presentations, or in the time it may take to prepare an individual one (see Idea 88).

88

BE PREPARED

EVERY TEXT ABOUT selling stresses the need for preparation, and the danger of trying to "wing it." Yet there are occasions when many salespeople do just that. They think they have everything in mind, and that no further thought is necessary. This area is so important that one example to stress the dangers is a must.

The idea

From a firm of architects . . .

This particular firm was already successful, but it wanted to increase the size of projects for which it was invited to pitch. It went for a job involving the building of residential training centers for a national charity, and after preliminary meetings, was put on the shortlist. This firm and two others then had to make a presentation to the board that ran the charity. This necessitated some preparation. Three people were to speak; they met briefly and shared out the task, and one of them agreed to make the slides they would use in the presentation.

Given the nature of the business, there were impressive things to show, and slides were always an important part of any pitch for an architecture firm. The three met again briefly on the evening before the presentation, and looked through the chosen slides. The following morning they arrived at the charity's London headquarters ten minutes ahead of their allotted time. A secretary showed them to a conference room, and one of them asked where the power point was so they could set up the laptop and projector they had brought with them.

It was only when the secretary expressed amazement that the truth dawned on them: they were in the offices of the Royal National Institute for the Blind. As the secretary said, "All the people attending the meeting have impaired sight and most are totally blind." Really, it had not occurred to them. They had done all their preparation on automatic pilot, and chosen slides because it was what they always did. They showed every potential client examples of recent work. Two minutes later they made the presentation with no slides, and did not win the contract.

In practice

- Never try to just "wing it."

- Accept that preparation is necessary, not least to tailor what you do to the individual circumstances. It matters. It must be done. It makes a difference. It may take a couple of minutes or a couple of hours, perhaps in discussion with colleagues, but the rule should be: always prepare carefully.

THE POWER OF DESCRIPTION

EVERYONE IN SELLING must know the concept of features and benefits, and that, to use an old phrase, you sell the sizzle and not the sausages. People buy something because of what it does for them, or means to them; that is, they buy because of its benefits. As a result, sales messages should predominantly be benefit-led: you talk about the benefits, and use the features as factors that demonstrate how a benefit can be delivered. So far so good, yet prevailing practice is by no means perfect, and the world is full of salespeople busily talking about features. Certainly I find that significant numbers of people attending courses on sales techniques do not really understand the difference between features and benefits.

Even when you clearly understand the difference, the way benefits are described is a key factor in making a successful sales pitch and obtaining agreement.

The idea

From a manufacturer of catering equipment . . .

Selling a range of cookers, grills, water heaters, and other items for hotels, restaurants, and various such establishments certainly involves a degree of technical detail, but let's just concentrate on a couple of simple facts. Imagine too that a busy café is the intended customer.

One feature of a flat grill is its size. Say the model being sold has a cooking area of 800 square centimeters. Perhaps not many people can instantly imagine what that looks like. But if you say it can cook a dozen eggs simultaneously (*because* it has an 800 sq cm surface area), and tie this in to the "rush at breakfast time," everyone in the catering business will be able to call a picture instantly to mind, and see the advantage.

Similarly, to sell a twin 8 pint water heater, you would do best not to emphasize the 8 pint capacity, but to refer to its ability to dispense both tea and coffee at the same time.

Descriptions like this, which are not only benefit-oriented, but also focused on the customer's specific situation, are worth a great deal. They link to the customers' experience, and prompt their imagination. I could probably give 99 more examples of this kind of thing, and fill up the rest of the book with them, but that might not make for the most helpful of manuals.

In practice

- Bland or inappropriate description—lazy description, if you like—can dilute a good case to the point where it will persuade no one.

- Good, powerful descriptions, as described above, are, however, a prerequisite of successful selling. This is something every salesperson needs to work at to get right.

90 A TELLING SONG

THE IDEA HERE is important, but the example that brought it to mind is not strictly a sales one. First, some brief background: I have recently written a travel book (*First Class at Last!*, Marshall Cavendish), which focuses on a journey from Singapore to Bangkok on the luxury Eastern & Oriental Express. This involved a visit to Singapore, where one evening I went to Harry's Bar, a well-known jazz venue on Boat Quay.

The idea

From jazz singer Marina Xavier . . .

At around 9pm every evening, Harry's Bar presents live music. There is a resident band, but the night I was there a guest artist was appearing, Eurasian songstress Marina Xavier. (She had an album to promote, so she was selling, in a sense.) Let me give her a plug: she's very good, and if you like cool jazz, the album is *When the World was Young* (available on Amazon, if Singapore is off your route).

One of the last things Marina said by way of introduction was, "What day is it today?" Someone shouted "Tuesday." "OK," she said, "let's make it seem like Friday night." And she was off into the first song. Wittingly or not, she did two things that every salesperson should always do early in any sales encounter. First, she showed an interest in her audience (customers), demonstrating that she cared about how they felt, and wanted them to feel good. Second, she did this in a pleasant and light way, which (was one of the things that) put people at their ease.

In practice

- The two things above go together. No one will buy easily if they feel a salesperson is not interested in them (or their product), yet this feeling has to be introduced easily and comfortably, and not in a way that is labeled, "Notice that I'm interested in you!" Sometimes a focus on the job to be done and the facts that must be put over allows this kind of finesse inadvertently to be omitted.

- Never forget that the feeling between a customer and a salesperson contributes to the outcome of the meeting, and act accordingly.

NOT ONLY ARE some customers different from others (it has already been stressed here that customers need individual treatment); some are also larger than others, in terms of either business received from them or potential. A big customer is sometimes satisfyingly and gratefully simply labeled "big," and no further action is taken. But if the volume of business is already large, that does not mean it cannot be increased. There is an old saying that even the best performance can be improved, and despite the apparent contradiction, this is a sensible attitude to take.

The idea

Analyzing the potential of major customers . . .

There is a whole separate literature on major accounts, and on the management of the relationships that go with them (something to investigate if you have such customers). Here, however, is one idea that can quickly create new business possibilities. I like it because in its simplest form it can be worked out on the back of an envelope (even using approximate figures).

The necessary analysis simply takes the value of a large customer's business and splits the figure across two axes of a matrix. One axis lists products (or product areas) one by one, and the other lists buying points one by one. For example, for my own business I could list consulting, training (or perhaps several separate areas of training: sales, making presentations, business writing), and writing. Then I could list the various buying points in a client company. There are various ways to do this, but in my case I'd probably opt for function—the marketing department, HR, and more—or location: for instance offices in London and Manchester, or London, New York, and Singapore.

In practice

How is this useful?

- If you do this, you'll find some boxes of the matrix show a higher value than others. A great deal of product A might be sold in London, but (surprisingly?) little of product B, for instance.

- Or there might be total gaps—nothing being sold in particular areas of a large customer's organization.

- Asking why can identify opportunities and provide targets for future selling. Maybe there are new contacts to be investigated; maybe you can get an introduction from one part of the company to another.

- Exploring the details in this way almost always provides some food for thought. Just saying, "These figures are good," doesn't help you identify how they could be still better.

NO PROBLEM

As I WRITE this I am arranging a training course for a large multinational IT company, to be held in its office in Singapore. (I work there regularly.) With participants assembling from five countries, and an HR manager who keeps tinkering with the agenda, there are many arrangements to be made. This is a new client, and one with potential for the future. One thing about this situation illustrates an important principle.

The idea

When circumstances pose some difficulty . . .

There are two potential difficulties in this situation, which both link to the fact that my clients and I are some 6,000 miles apart, and I want to ensure that this does not look in any way inconvenient at the client end. First, there is the question of language. My prime contact is Thai, and although he speaks good English, the potential for misunderstanding is greater than would be the case if we had the same first language. I need to take care, and just a little more thought and time than usual, to avoid any ambiguousness, and make sure everything is clear as we go along.

Second, there is a time difference between the two locations. If I have an email in the morning, then I have only until about 11am to reply before the office day ends in Singapore. This is not always convenient; but it is important. I want my contacts to be seen as efficient—and it helps me too to get matters agreed and not extend the time it takes to do so. So I have to do some juggling to make this possible.

None of this is too difficult, but it does need some thought. Any such awkwardness must always be handled carefully. We have no inalienable right to sell or deal with our customers in a way that maximizes the convenience to us. In this case, if I want to work in that part of the world, I have to adjust a little to make it possible and make it work.

In practice

- It can be easy in a busy life, and with demands always seeming to conflict, to find that we are unthinkingly putting ourselves first in various logistical ways.

- But, whatever awkwardness you may face, it is a good idea to put the customer first. Only if the relationship works for them are they likely to see it as advantageous; and only then will they buy.

93 BECAUSE YOU'RE SPECIAL

THERE IS A saying that a little flattery goes a long way, meaning that flattery can oil the wheels of relationships, and carry people with you. Of course, this is something to use carefully. If flattery is used like a blunt instrument, or in the wrong context, it will simply rub people up the wrong way. Besides, many people think they are not susceptible to flattery, and perhaps the more sophisticated are not. If you have just said to yourself, "Quite right, I can spot flattery coming at ten paces and it doesn't fool me," then you have just proved the point that it *does* work.

The idea

From an international conference organizer . . .

I was recently asked to be a keynote speaker at an international conference to be held in Seoul. Although the organizer offered to cover the costs of travel and accommodation, the fee was small, and I needed to be there for the three days the event lasted. So allowing for my travel time, I wasn't going to make much money for the time it would take me. The organizer used two major tactics to persuade me to participate. First, the event would attract interesting people, and be a notable networking event at which I might forge new contacts and profitable alliances. This was certainly a consideration: I thought it might well be useful, especially since I work regularly in Southeast Asia, and delegates would attend from around the region.

Second, the organizer used a considerable amount of flattery. She praised to the skies my expertise, my knowledge of the topic—and my book on the subject. She made it clear that without my presence the conference would only be a pale shadow of what it might have been if I were to be involved. Now logically I know that it would (sadly) run perfectly well without me, but it is difficult not to respond to this kind of thing. If they really think this, I should be well looked after . . . If they . . . I could see perfectly well what was being done here (flattery costs less than paying a higher fee!), but it certainly had an effect.

In practice

- Flattery works in many situations. It does not guarantee a sale, of course (what does?), but it can put just a little more weight on the positive side of the balance

- Regard flattery as a useful tool in your armory, but you do need to use it carefully. I'm sure you already know that, so of course you will.

94

THE SMALL PRINT

MANY A DEAL has foundered on the small print. The customer likes the product, they want to buy the product, maybe even at some stage they actually intend to do so, then—suddenly—they decline. Something about the terms of the deal destroyed their intent.

The idea

From the conference industry . . .

The terms and conditions you state for contracts must protect your financial position as supplier, and in particular, protect your profitability. At the same time it is important that they:

- Are communicated clearly and prevent misunderstandings.

- Project efficiency.

- Enhance the client relationship (for which they must be seen as acceptable and necessary).

- Encourage conversion of business effectively and promptly.

- Link to any other necessary arrangements and documentation.

I first worked on the detail of what is best here during some research with the Meetings Industry Association. The key here and elsewhere is that when discussing terms and conditions you should never apologize. Stress the mutual advantages of clearly specified contract conditions. Talk about working together, and if necessary use a checklist to ensure you deal with everything systematically. Specifically you may want to evolve a step-by-step way of introducing and describing terms and conditions, and making them stick. This is the kind of progression involved:

- Introduce the concept of contractual agreement. You need to consider the timing of this in the context of your type of business, but it is usually best early on rather than later.

- Make clear the detail. You must be careful to spell it out accurately, and not assume the customer is familiar with everything, least of all figures, costings, and timing. Always check understanding (this may need only a simple question).

- Document your side of the arrangements. Tell the customer what you will do, and follow it up efficiently and promptly in a way that sets the pattern for clear written communications. Make it easy for the customer (you set out the details), but ask for confirmation, chase if necessary to get it, and keep clear records throughout the process if it takes any amount of time.

In practice

- Adopt the appropriate manner throughout the process, and make it clear that none of this is a negative procedure.

- Stress the advantages to the customer of having things clear. Link to any follow-up, and ultimately this includes invoicing. (Here it is most important that the invoice reflects—accurately—the agreed detail, and is straightforward and clear.)

95

BENCHMARK YOURSELF

YOU MAY BE pretty good at selling (even though you say so yourself), but do you know how you compare with others, not just in your own organization, but also more widely?

The idea

From consultants Miller Heiman . . .

This company specializes in the sales area. It does regular research, and one survey, conducted in conjunction with Quest Media Ltd, and published in the journal *Winning Business*, reviewed current practice and looked to the future. It examined the changing sales role, customer expectations and beliefs, and the whole way sales teams are organized, staffed, rewarded, and managed.

Key findings indicated that:

- Customers are becoming better informed and more organized, demanding, and sharp in their dealings with salespeople (with the internet being used to a significant extent for pre-buying research).

- Technology is having, and will continue to have, an effect on sales activity. Most dramatically it is replacing salespeople with electronic, impersonal buying, although this is not affecting large numbers of business areas. The dynamic nature of this area is evidenced by the uncertainty respondents reflected in their forecasts of what other influences are becoming important.

- Recruitment is a perpetual challenge, as is retention.

- CRM is becoming a more widespread basis for many customer interactions, and creating a more formal basis for them.

- Training remains a constant need (and more of it is being done, and the range of ways in which it is done are also increasing), as the level of competency of salespeople is seen as key to success.

- Reporting takes a high proportion of working time, reducing salespeople's time spent face to face with customers. This is despite the increasing computerization of data collection and reporting systems.

In practice

- Such an examination is likely to be useful to any organization wondering whether its sales operation is maximizing opportunities. (Maybe one day it will be updated.)

- Any opportunity to examine and learn about how other people operate should be taken; such information is likely to be useful to any organization or any individual.

- At best one fact that emerges, as with the ideas here, could be adopted or adapted, and change your own practice for the better.

96

SHOW TO SELL

SOMETIMES, WITH SOME products, you do better not to talk about something, but to show it—demonstrate it—working. Whether it is a photocopier or a car in which you offer prospects a test drive, the principles are similar.

The idea

Many people do less than a good job of demonstrating. But here I have in mind Panasonic, and a perfectly conducted demo of theirs I once attended . . .

What are the key factors if a demonstration is to work and boost the chances of sales success? Many of the basic rules of selling apply here. You must focus on needs, maintain interest (maybe not every aspect of your offering will be of the same level of interest to your customers, and a comprehensive run-through of features may be neither necessary nor appreciated), go through matters following a pre-explained structure and sequence, and above all, talk benefits. The job is to get people to imagine something in use. So remember:

- Set up fast. Make sure you get everything ready. Have you got the key and is the electricity switched on?

- Make it understandable. This is vital. Demonstrations can be spoiled by jargon, gobbledegook, and confusion. Sometimes they consist of an over-lengthy discussion about irrelevant details. Everything must be spelled out so that it is crystal clear. If your prospect finds it easy to understand, that is a good sign. Prompts to imagination can quickly build up a powerful picture.

- It must work! If anything fails to work as you say it should, then from the customer's point of view you have a problem, and quite right too. The experience must be smooth as silk.

- Make them feel how it could be. Everything must be done not just so they "get a feeling for something" in a general sense, but also so they can truly imagine how it would be to own and use the product.

- Project what you want—and what the customer wants. If the customer has asked you to demonstrate something specific, make sure you show how your offering will meet their needs.

In practice

- Throughout the process of demonstrating, the main emphasis is on proof. You are not just talking about your offering, you can show it, and the prospect can try it—and seeing is believing.

- You must work to ensure everything is exactly as you want. There are very few second chances in selling, and in few parts of the process is this truer than when you demonstrate something in this way.

- Time spent beforehand to make sure that you get it right is time very well spent.

97

DEFINE YOUR JOB

DIFFERENT SALES JOBS are, well, different. For instance, one may involve much cold calling, another none. One may involve short one-off meetings, while others may necessitate a long chain of events all of which must be got right. Simply to say that the job is "to sell" is not a useful guide to making it successful.

The idea

From American business guru Mark McCormack . . .

For selling to be done well, anyone doing it must be clear what "doing selling" means. The first step here is to produce a clear definition of your own sales job. This needs to be entirely job and organization-specific, but general overviews can be helpful here too. For instance the following comes from *On Selling*, a book by Mark McCormack, the American sports marketing consultant and commentator:

The qualities that I believe make a good salesperson:

- Believe in your product

- Believe in yourself

- See a lot of people

- Pay attention to timing

- Listen to the customer—but realize that what the customer wants is not necessarily what he or she is telling you

- Develop a sense of humor

- Knock on old doors

- Ask everyone to buy

- Follow up after the sale with the same aggressiveness you demonstrated before the sale

- Use common sense

I have no illusions that I'm breaking new ground with this list. These are essential, self-evident, universal qualities that all salespeople know in their heads—if not in their hearts.

Well said.

In practice

- Whatever your job entails and however many different aspects of it there may be, you need to be clear about it all.

- Furthermore you need to be clear about how different tasks fit together, to know what you have to do to be sure of doing a good job. If half your job is cold canvassing, make sure that you spend 50 percent of your time talking to new prospects, and so on, as your job dictates.

- It is surprising how often salespeople take all this as read. They know the job they must do, but if a lack of analysis means that they fail to give a correct emphasis to any specific part of the job, then they may be in trouble. Good definition underpins good practice.

98

GO ON FOOT

I'VE MENTIONED SALES productivity elsewhere. It is a truism that the greater the amount of time you spend—primarily face to face—with customers, the greater the chances of your concluding deals and producing business. Yet there are so many hazards that can easily act to dilute productivity and reduce time spent with customers. Administration is just one factor.

If you see five customers each working day (and some see fewer), then given about 220 working days in the year (allowing for holidays, sickness, sales meetings, and more), you make not many more than 1,000 calls a year—and there is a great deal to do in that time, no doubt. It's a scary thought.

The idea

From those organizations with the fittest salespeople . . .

There is one factor almost guaranteed to increase productivity, and yet shunned by some (many?) salespeople. That is to do with cars. Given the increasingly slow speed of traffic in most major cities, salespeople the world over spend more and more of their time traveling. Time spent in the car is essentially non-productive. It might seem that there is comparatively little to be done about this, but some companies have banned salespeople from moving around by car in core city centers. It may be a revolutionary thought, but you should consider *getting out of the car and walking*.

In practice

- Some organizations that suggest or demand this expect to see a receipt for parking. This acts as proof that salespeople really are walking (or jumping on a bus perhaps) from one central contact to another. Although it often seems quicker to drive, many are surprised by how much time this saves.

- This is not always a good idea (some salespeople simply have too much to carry), but for many it is well worth a thought, at least for some of their working days. And traffic seems to get worse day by day.

BEFORE WE END . . .

Now FOR TWO ideas are a little different in nature, though potentially as useful as any other. They catalogue a few things not to do: things that do nothing to make success more likely, rub customers up the wrong way, or are simply self-defeating. This list could be much longer (maybe it could fill another book?), and still document things that are seen all too commonly. It is a testament to two things. First, the prevailing standards of selling are not so high, and second, this fact is indicative of an opportunity—those that excel do well.

NEVER TELL OBVIOUS LIES

It may be that selling involves some exaggeration, and occasionally a little white lie, but more than that runs risks. Tell someone that the battery life of some gizmo is twice what it actually is, and this description may help clinch the sale, but it may also mean the customer is back promptly to return the goods, and resolves never to buy from you again.

Yet despite the logic of this, some salespeople not only tell lies, they compound the damage by telling obvious lies, in some cases making statements that are both cliché and spotted as doubtful at ten paces. My least favorite, and a common one, is the salesperson seeking an appointment who says something like, "What about Tuesday morning at 10 am? I will be in your area then." Now, not only do I not believe this for a single second (the person will be in my area only if I agree to a meeting), strangely I do not see helping the person to reduce their travel time as a priority at this early stage in our relationship. Certainly it is not a reason to see them. Such a line simply fails to reflect the realities of the relationship.

The idea

For all salespeople overrating their own convenience . . .

Do not say this, or indeed any other permutation of it. Not ever. Certainly do not offer it baldly as a reason that someone should see you. If a prospect agrees to a meeting, if you have persuaded them to take an initial interest, then by all means try to make meeting them productive. If you want to offer a time that is easy for you (rather than asking them what suits them best), at least be honest about it, and position it as helping you. They may well be helpful: having agreed to see you, they may well not want to appear awkward. But express the thought too early and in the wrong way, and you create the reverse of the impression you want.

In practice

- Nothing creates negative feelings in a customer about a salesperson faster than this sort of thing.

- Avoid it.

WHY ARE YOU CALLING?

THIS BOOK HAS touched on one of the perennial success factors of selling: preparation. Good records, clear thinking before a sales meeting, an agenda, and more, all help you to run the kind of meeting that you want, and that customers find useful. One fault I have seen more regularly than any other over the years is linked to this idea. It is somehow perpetuated by being rationalized as "useful."

The idea

For all salespeople who do not think through the reason for calling . . .

If I had even a modestly valued coin of the realm for every time the words "courtesy call" have appeared on salespeople's call report forms, under a heading like "Reason for call," I would be a millionaire. Let me be clear immediately: *there should be no such thing as a courtesy call.*

Every call needs specific objectives. It is not useful, least of all to productivity, to call because it is a month since you saw someone last, because you can fit a call in easily en route somewhere else, or worst of all, to make up the number of calls needed to hit the target for a particular week. You must be able to spell out tangible reasons for the call, and not least to express them in customer terms—saying what *they* will get from the call that is useful.

In practice

- Of course there are certain calls that are less directly related than others to getting an order. Some refer to these as public relations calls. But if you are seeing someone as part of building a long-term relationship, or to set the scene for some future initiative, you need clear objectives for the specific visit.

- Calling something a courtesy call allows a lack of thought and planning to seem somehow justified: "It's just a courtesy call." If there is no real reason for the visit, something you can spell out in terms of clear objectives, do not make the call. Set objectives for a meeting with another prospect, and see them instead. Your sales will benefit.

FINALLY (A STORY)

ONCE THERE WAS a fairground strongman. One trick in his act was to take an orange and place it in the crook of his arm. He would then bend his arm and squeeze all the juice out of the orange. Once this was done he would challenge the audience, offering a cash prize to anyone who could get a further drop out of the mangled orange.

One day after many people had tried and failed, one apparently unlikely candidate came forward. He was the very opposite of the strongman, slight and feeble looking, but he took his turn, squeezed and squeezed . . . and finally succeeded in getting a further drop of juice out of the orange.

The strongman and the audience were amazed. The strongman handed over the money, and wondering how this had been possible, asked what the man did for a living. "I'm a buyer with the Ford Motor Company," he said.

Note: If you sell components to the motor industry this will certainly ring bells, but it is the kind of apocryphal story that can be told and linked to any organization you have in mind. When I was told this first, it was followed by the comment, "Not all buyers are like that. Some are worse." And yours?

Whatever product or service you sell, the attitude you take to selling will certainly influence the level of success you achieve.

- Never forget that the most important part of the sales equation is the customer.

- Never, ever underestimate customers.

- To sell successfully you must respect them and their position in the buying/selling process; and have plenty of good ideas to help convince them.

KEEP SEARCHING FOR AN EDGE

As a FINAL entry (and yes, I know it says 100 ideas on the cover, but I have made a point of emphasizing the usefulness of something unexpected), I would like to make a point about the dynamic nature of the sales process. Sadly there is no one magic bullet that transforms every sales situation into a certain winner. Every salesperson must get used to some rejection, and work with the prevailing strike rate in their industry. What this book does is provide ideas that might improve your strike rate. The best salespeople never give up on the process of improvement. They see the process as dynamic, and constantly work to better what they do.

Not every skill is like this. Something that illustrates this principle, one that occurs to me as I write, is the skill of typing. I may type less than perfectly, but I do use a lot of fingers, and I do go at a fair rate. (Publishers do not pay enough to make slow writing economic!) This is something of a static skill. As long as I do enough typing, and do so regularly, my speed will keep up, and I do not really have to learn anything new—unless the querty keyboard is superseded. But it must be borne in mind that selling is certainly not like that. What needs to be done with one customer today is different from what must be done with another (or even the same one) next week, next month, or next year.

Idea 101

From motor giant BMW . . .

I mention this company because of its conspicuous success. This is a respected worldwide organization, one that sells a very large numbers of cars every year; it is no stretch of the imagination to think that its salespeople must be no slouches. Yet BMW constantly refreshes the skills of its people. I have written several different books about aspects of selling, and the largest single order I have ever had for one title (actually *The Sales Excellence Pocketbook*, published by Management Pocketbooks) was for very nearly a thousand copies—from BMW.

In practice

- Whatever ideas you use, or adapt and use, from this volume, never stop searching for new ones. Sales success is not a matter of luck, so I will not wish you good luck, but I wish you well with it.

AFTERWORD

THERE IS ALWAYS something new to be done in selling. There are many maxims about aiming high, and "positive mental attitude" is not just a state of mind, it is an industry, certainly in America. This is all so obvious, but the dangers are equally real. It is very easy to form clear intentions to achieve excellence, take some action, but allow an initial lack of success and the ongoing pressure of work to let you sideline them, and do little or nothing more. Sustaining a program of review and progress needs some commitment and some persistence.

If you aim high, you may still not achieve the peak of success, but you are likely to achieve more than you would with lower intentions. There are four manifestations of this:

- Excellence: In terms of everything you do and the professionalism with which you do it, you should aim for excellence. In selling, getting by is never enough. Unless you are ahead of the game, unless you are constantly moving forward, you are vulnerable to changing circumstances, and what you do may no longer impress customers as it should. In a dynamic environment the status quo is an enemy. As Henry Kaiser said, "You can't sit on the lid of progress. If you do, you will be blown to pieces."

- Challenge: You should not rule things out too readily as being beyond you. Only by accepting a challenge will you make progress, and in any case more job satisfaction comes from taking on and making a success of something genuinely challenging than from just "ticking over" and allowing a job to become repetitive. In selling, it also gets you more business.

- Advancement: Success in your current job and in your longer-term career comes, in part at least, from how you perform. If you fail to try new ideas and approaches, you may effectively block your progress, and regret it later. Sales, and sales careers, thrive on the application of new ideas.

- Skills and techniques: To do a particular job, you need to be able to do, and do well, the things that it necessitates. So you need to take on the challenge of developing new skills. Such things often seem daunting. There was a stage in my career when the last thing I ever thought I would do, or wanted to do, or indeed thought I would be able to do, was public speaking. I hated the very idea. But circumstances led me toward it. I had to learn how to do it—and have in fact spent a major part of my subsequent career in training in speaking to groups of all sizes, and indeed teaching others to do so. So you must not rule out areas of development for the wrong reasons, and these include distaste for them, and a lack of confidence in your ability to do them. Aiming high includes embracing the acquisition of all the skills that will take you where you want to go. This may mean getting your head around one new sales technique or approach, or moving into a whole new area of work.

Certainly all this demands a positive attitude. If you think you can, you can, and if you think you can't, you're right (according to Mary Kay Ash). Fair comment. So be positive about your selling, and your ability to satisfy customers. Be positive about your ability to succeed and make progress. Of course, as this text has made clear, you need to work at the sales process, and do so in a considered and systematic way. Success does not just happen, but you can make it happen, and your attitude to and action in terms of reviewing current practice and taking it forward provides the foundations for tomorrow's sales success.

One new idea may take you a step forward in terms of results and customer satisfaction; a steady stream of them will secure your future.

OTHER 100 GREAT IDEAS

100 Great Business Ideas
From leading companies around the world
Jeremy Kourdi

Know how to prepare a deep-dive prototype? How's your social networking? And are you up to speed in your psychographic profiling and vendor lock-in procedures?

In the world of business, new ideas and energy are needed constantly—in many ways and at varying times—to ensure success. This book contains 100 insightful and useful business ideas that will help you succeed.

Written in a stimulating and flexible way, *100 Great Business Ideas* contains ideas with proven power and potency that actually work. The ideas are varied, interesting, and thought-provoking, and some of the best ideas used in business. Some are simple—sometimes almost embarrassingly so—while others are based on detailed research and brilliant intellect.

If you have a restless desire and the energy to do well and stay ahead of the competition and a willingness to experiment and take a risk, this book will inspire you to find out more or develop your thinking along new, creative lines, generating brilliant ideas for the future.

ISBN 978-0-462-09960-6 / £8.99 PAPERBACK

OTHER 100 GREAT IDEAS

100 Great Copywriting Ideas
From leading companies around the world
Andy Maslen

Do you use the biggest cliché in the copywriter's toolkit? What's more important than optimizing web copy for search engines? And how do you start a headline promising practical information?

Once defined as salesmanship in print, and now, by the author of this book, as selling in print and on screen, copywriting takes your message to the masses. Or maybe just to the 23 individuals worldwide you need to communicate with.

Get it right and you can sit back and count the money. But getting it right isn't easy. Sure you can fill the page—or screen—with words that *describe* your product, and even your delight in having "totally redesigned our website" but that won't translate into sales. This book helps you turn what you know about your product and, hopefully, your reader, into powerful selling copy that shifts merchandise.

100 Great Copywriting Ideas is more tapas or dim sum than three-course meal. You can start anywhere you like and pick and choose whatever takes your fancy. The book brims with 100 self-contained ideas from companies as varied as Hamleys, Time Out, Malmaison, Waitrose, Crocus.co.uk and Porsche. Author Andy Maslen, says, "Ideas are the lifeblood of great copy. Here are 100 of mine you can transfuse into your own writing."

ISBN 978-0-462-09973-6 / £8.99 PAPERBACK